Developing

I0013114

Quarterly

MAKING ORGANIZATIONS MORE HUMAN

Augmented Intelligence

Catalyzing your leadership practice

Publisher's note

Every effort has been made to ensure information contained in this publication is accurate at the time of going to press. Neither the publishers nor any of the contributors can accept responsibility for any errors or omissions, however caused, nor for any loss or damage occasioned to any person acting, or refraining from action, as a result of the material in this publication.

Users and readers of this publication may copy portions of the material for personal use, internal reports, or reports to clients provided that such articles (or portions of articles) are attributed to this publication by name, the individual contributor of the portion uses and publisher.

IEDP Ideas for Leaders Ltd
42 Moray Place, Edinburgh, EH3 6BT
www.ideasforleaders.com

in association with the Center for the Future of Organization at the Drucker School of Management
www.futureorg.org

Publishers: Roland Deiser and Roddy Millar
Editor-in-Chief: Roddy Millar
Senior Editor: Roland Deiser
Associate Editors: Saar Ben-Attar (Africa), Suzie Lewis (Europe) Conrado Schlochauer (LatAm), Ravi Shankar (SE Asia)
Art Direction: Nick Mortimer – nickmortimer.co.uk

ISBN 978-1-91-552938-1 (Paperback)
ISBN 978-1-91-552939-8 (e-Pub)
ISSN 2044-2203 (Developing Leaders Quarterly)

www.developingleadersquarterly.com

Contents

The world is awash with the buzz of AI. What it can do for us, why everything will change because of it, why we should fear it and how we need to control it. As with other technological developments, the impact it will make is less to do with the technology and more to do with how we, as humans, embrace it.

The Internet and smartphones have revolutionized our world, making today's life materially different to that of 30 years ago, this is more to do with their accessibility, low-cost and user-friendliness than the strength of technological computing power they embody. Other technologies have failed to have such wide impact, virtual reality or self-driving cars for example, as we have not been able to get them to a stage of mass accessibility yet. They remain in the zone of early adopters and tech-geeks.

AI shows every sign of being in the former camp. ChatGPT and its competitors are ever-easier to use and access, and as a result a plethora of new apps and services are appearing. We find ourselves using these services without any great understanding of the tech that lies behind them, though often we can still detect where the hand of AI has taken over.

For this issue, our brilliant art director for DLQ, Nick Mortimer, exclusively used AI-generated images for all the chapter title pages. They are rich in detail and content and would have taken him many hours to create himself, but you can sense they are not entirely his own work. They have a homogeneity and perhaps lack some sense of soul, that his normal selections and adaptations offer.

However, as Terry Sejnowski notes in his book 'ChatGPT and the Future of AI' (reviewed on p188), we are at an equivalent stage in technical development with AI, as the Wright brothers were with flight – huge advances lie ahead of us. The technology will evolve transactionally, each new development will build on the knowledge and expertise that precedes it; but the impact that technology can make will be factored on how we find ourselves using it. As always, it is the human element that will dictate its success.

And that is what we explore in this issue. The extraordinary abilities, both current and fast-approaching, that AI can bring are in every newspaper, blog and magazine; what is less examined is what we need to do to utilize these abilities. What mindsets we should adopt to make the most of these abilities, how we need to rethink the structure of organizations to accommodate digital co-workers, how we can manage work and workflows in this new age. Ultimately, what will the role of the human, and in particular the human leader, be in this new paradigm?

These are the questions, both philosophical as well as practical, that we set out to explore in this issue. We do not necessarily find clear answers, but the act of discussion, reflection and exploration of these topics is hugely valuable in aligning our understanding and progressing our thinking. I doubt the Wright brothers imagined the enormity and ubiquity of the airline industry today – or ever considered its environmental impact; but the evolution of AI will be much swifter than that of airplanes.

We have called this issue 'Augmented Intelligence' as it is really about how AI (artificial intelligence) can interact with us humans, and the collaboration and relationship we need to develop to optimize our world with this new power. It is entirely possible that AI will shift the world dramatically, but it will only happen beneficially if we learn to use it wisely – and quickly. It must augment us not replace us.

We have the usual breadth of contributions to stimulate your thinking in this issue, from Tom Davenport, the distinguished professor of IT and Management at Babson College, to Rimma Boshernitsan a futurist and strategist and CEO of Dialogue and Eve Psalti, senior director at Microsoft's Azure AI engineering, plus plenty of others.

We're sure you will find plenty to provoke and inspire your leadership thinking.

Roddy Millar, Editorial Director and Co-publisher
Roland Deiser, Co-publisher

Thinking imprinted.

The first step in leadership development is creating space for reflection on your practice.

Studies show we absorb information better from print, which allows focused, uninterrupted reading and the ability to jot down thoughts.

To embed the change, Developing Leaders Quarterly is best in print. The print edition is conveniently sized to slip into your pocket, bag, or briefcase, making it easy to read in spare moments—whether commuting, at the airport, or before a meeting.

By Thomas H. Davenport

AI and Human Jobs

Where Are We Now, and What Should Leaders Do?

The issue of how artificial intelligence will affect human work is one of the most popular, but perhaps the least well understood, of any aspect of AI. The high visibility of this issue alone, along with other rational reasons for concern, makes it an issue that leaders need to address head-on. Surveys suggest that CEOs see AI as a transformative force for their organizations, and many say they plan to reduce headcount because of it. Yet many CEOs and HR leaders have not articulated clear views on what they believe will happen to their human employees as a result of AI, which employees will be most affected, and how they should be preparing for the transition.

For over a decade I have been researching and writing about the issue of how AI will affect work and human workers. Like anyone who pays close attention to this fast-changing technology, I have had a few changes in perspective over the years. I have gone from pessimistic to optimistic to guarded based on what I have read, what I have observed and studied in actual workplaces, and what I have seen and anticipate in terms of changes in AI technology.

From Pessimism to Optimism on the Future of Human Employment

What I have read from other authors has largely made me more pessimistic. When I began to study AI and work, I read several books (including *Rise of the Robots* and *Humans Need Not Apply*, both published in 2015) that were largely speculative and negative about the long-term prospects for human employment. They made me quite pessimistic about human job prospects in the face of AI advances. In addition, the Oxford Martin Institute study of *The Future of Employment* had been published in 2013, and it appeared to be rigorous in its methodology— breaking jobs down into tasks and analyzing whether the tasks could be done by smart machines. It posited that 47% of US jobs were at risk of elimination from AI-driven automation, and received much publicity for its findings.

I have gone from pessimistic to optimistic to guarded based on what I have read, what I have observed and studied in actual workplaces, and what I have seen and anticipate in terms of changes in AI technology.

But then Julia Kirby and I decided to write a Harvard Business Review article (nicely illustrated with photos of toy robots) and book on the subject. We began to interview managers and professionals about what they and their organizations were actually doing with and planning for AI. In that research we found very little evidence of large-scale automation and job elimination. We realized that most jobs consisted of many tasks, and only some of them could be automated with AI. Only in structured manufacturing environments, where each new robot displaces 3.3 human workers on average, has there been substantial job loss. Indeed, many companies have found it very difficult to hire the workers they need over the past several years.

When Kirby and I published a book about our findings in 2016, instead of suggesting that no humans need apply for work, we titled it *Only Humans Need Apply*. We argued that "augmentation"—humans and

Only in structured manufacturing environments, where each new robot displaces 3.3 human workers on average, has there been substantial job loss

machines working in combination—was both more likely and a better strategy for organizations in thinking about AI and work. It gives organizations more flexibility and ability to innovate, while still taking advantage of the speed and efficiency advantages of some automation. We discussed five different steps that humans can take to augment AI, the most common being for humans to "step in" and work directly in collaboration with AI. I believed this to be an optimistic perspective and held it for several years; nothing I observed in talking with many organizations made me feel that large-scale automation was on the immediate horizon.

I was further confirmed in this optimistic perspective a few years later, when I published a book in 2022 with Steven Miller called *Working with AI: Real Stories of Human-Machine Collaboration*. We felt that if people were going to be working alongside AI, they might benefit from some detailed examples of how that collaboration works out across multiple different work settings. The resulting book included 29 short case studies of how humans and

machines were collaborating on a daily basis. Almost all of them—with the possible exception of an automated but unreliable hamburger flipper—were working well for both employees and employers. Not a single incumbent of these 29 jobs expected that their role would be automated out of existence. In the discussion of the implications, we concluded, "We suspect that even with the relentless trajectory of improvement in AI capabilities, widespread augmentation is here to stay."

Predictions Have Been Wrong

Further contributing to my optimism on this topic was some research I compiled on predictions of how many human jobs would be lost or gained from AI. I

One other thing these predictions have in common is that they were all wrong—some by massive amounts, some by smaller ones.

reviewed nine predictions on the total number of jobs to be lost or gained, and eight on the percentage of jobs that would be automated or automatable. The predictions varied widely, but they had several things in common. They all predicted substantial job losses (from 1,800,000 to two billion). They all provided a date by which the jobs lost or gained would be realized, varying from 2018 to 2038. Most also said there would be some job gains from AI, although most predicted substantially more losses than gains. All predicted some moderate-to-substantial percentage of automated jobs—ranging from 5% to the aforementioned 47% from the Oxford study.

One other thing these predictions have in common is that they were all wrong—some by massive amounts, some by smaller ones. The extent of their inaccuracy for predictions after 2024 (and before the present as well), has yet to discovered, but I suspect they will be quite wrong as well. All predicted millions of jobs lost and some predicted millions of jobs gained, but there is no evidence that either has come to pass. There are no good data on how many jobs have been lost or gained because of AI, but there is also no evidence of large-scale job loss. In many industrialized countries around the world (the most likely to deploy AI), there is low unemployment and labour shortages in many professions. Fields that were described as being highly subject to automation—radiology, for example—have particular high levels of labour shortages.

The smart predictors revised their predictions over time—largely becoming less pessimistic. The McKinsey Global Institute, for example, predicted in 2017 that 50% of job activities could be automated by 2055 or earlier. The same organization predicted in 2018 that 15% of global workers would lose their jobs to automation by 2030. In elaborations on these predictions, however, the consultants reduced the number of jobs likely to be automated out of existence to 5%, based on contextual factors like the technical feasibility of automation, the costs of developing and deploying automation solutions, and labour market dynamics. Even 5%, of course, has turned out to be an overly high prediction.

Generative AI and the Coming Singularity

Any good gambler tries to cover his bets, however, and my co-authors and I did so. In the *Working with AI* book,

One encouraging aspect of generative AI to date is that effective use of it should require a "human in the loop."

for example, the last section of the last chapter was titled, "If the Singularity Comes, All Bets Are Off." Miller and I thought if "singularity" or "artificial general intelligence" (AGI) ever came about—AI systems that could do everything that humans do, only better and faster—it would be difficult for humans to compete in job markets. But we, like most other "experts," felt that the singularity would not arrive for several more decades. Martin Ford, an "AI futurist" with a strong belief in automation-related job loss, interviewed 23 technical AI experts in the book *Architects of Intelligence*. 18 of the experts made predictions about when the singularity would take place. The average of the predictions was 2099.

Because of generative AI, I am guarded about when AGI will come and what it will mean for jobs. A 2024 survey of a larger number of AI experts found that 50% now believe that AGI will take place by 2040. Generative AI as we currently experience it does not represent AGI, but it provides a strong hint of what superintelligent machines will be able to do in the relatively near future. It already can write, converse, or create images better than many humans, and it is still early days for the technology.

Content creators—like the Hollywood writers who went on strike in 2023 in part to keep generative AI out of their jobs—have a lot to fear from it. So do call centre agents, actors, commercial artists, entry-level lawyers, and many other job incumbents.

Despite these concerns, early concerns about generative AI quickly displacing large numbers of workers have begun to fade. For example, several journalistic organizations (including CNET and Sports Illustrated) that embraced the technology early on found that it made highly visible errors and antagonized human employees, and they backed away from broad use of it. And generative AI use does not seem to have increased productivity measurably thus far.

One encouraging aspect of generative AI to date is that effective use of it should require a "human in the loop." Given the possibility of hallucinations (really just bad predictions by these statistically-based models), it is important for humans to review the output of gen AI models to ensure accuracy. In addition, users of generative AI often need to add value to the generated content to ensure that it is interesting and useful as well as accurate. Given that gen AI is trained on existing online content, it is unlikely that outputs will be truly novel. That may be fine for some applications, but content creators need to realize when it is important to go beyond well-established ideas and formats. However, reviewing and editing generative AI output may not be a natural inclination for human users. In one study of knowledge work creation by MIT researchers, 68% of participants chose not to edit the output of a language model.

Although it is still early days for the technology, generative AI has not changed the employment situation much yet in large organizations. Many of the companies I speak with that are adopting generative AI for various use cases still say—at least for public consumption—that they are augmenting human labour with the technology, rather than eliminating it. The line usually goes, "We're freeing-up humans to perform the tasks that only humans can do," or something along those lines. That has been the consistent party line for many years now, and the low unemployment numbers in the U.S. would seem to support it. A few organizations, such as Klarna in Sweden, have stated that generative AI will lead to substantially lower employment in some jobs (customer service in their case), but they are evolving to it through attrition.

With other new technologies, history has been on the side of human workers. Previous technologies that threatened jobs—such as ATMs and Internet banking with regard to bank tellers—did not decrease the numbers of teller jobs, but only slowed their growth. In jobs like newspaper reporting, although having AI write stories penetrated the industry a decade ago (particularly at the Associated Press, which recently struck a deal with OpenAI to collaborate on generative AI-written stories), the decline of newspaper advertising was a bigger factor in job loss. Generative AI may speed the decline of this and other waning professions, but I doubt it will be dramatic.

What we will see happen quickly, however, is that many jobs will involve working with AI as a collaborator or, as it is frequently called today, a "copilot." I have long believed that the only people who will lose their jobs to AI in the near term will be those jobholders who refuse to work with AI. They will be left behind as AI makes

human workers in many jobs more productive and effective. Those who work alongside AI will have to adopt new
skills and behaviours, but as long as they are flexible they
are likely to remain employed.

What Should Leaders Do?

Generative AI portends a scarier future, and the time
is now for leaders to begin to speak and act about that
future. The transformation of work by AI will, I believe, be
more gradual than dramatic, but it will also take years for
organizations and employees to fully prepare themselves.
There are several key steps that they can take today.

One step for social and political leaders is to help
threatened workers prepare themselves for the future.
Over the long-term successor versions of the already-im-

We should begin to prepare now for providing humans with money to live on and something useful to do when there are no longer enough jobs that only humans can do well.

pressive generative AI tools we have today are likely to hasten the pace of job loss. We should begin to prepare now for providing humans with money to live on and something useful to do when there are no longer enough jobs that only humans can do well.

Business leaders need to realize and communicate that business processes and tasks with "a human in the loop" are more likely to be successful than those that are fully automated. With generative AI, they need to encourage critical thinking and human review of AI output. Announcing that augmentation—not large-scale automation—will be the primary approach to AI will address workers' fears and give them the confidence to embrace AI in their own jobs.

Practically everyone within organizations will benefit from learning about how AI works and what its strengths and vulnerabilities are. This will help us all to become an effective colleague to AI systems. High-quality education on AI will be targeted to specific business functions and, in some cases, even jobs. Some companies, like Rack-

space, have already trained every worker on AI. Some states, including California, are embarking upon large-scale worker training on AI as well.

Organizational leaders should also address what types of jobs will become collaborative with AI, and in what ways. There are at least nine different options for how humans and smart machines can work together. In some cases, for example, the human takes the first pass at a task and the machine reviews it; in others the human has the last word. Begin to think about which options are most appropriate for key roles, and to train people in them for the relevant type of collaboration.

Finally, the question of how AI will affect a large organization's workforce is a complex and multi-faceted one that no individual leader can resolve alone. Executives should therefore put a group together to address the

In some cases, for example, the human takes the first pass at a task and the machine reviews it; in others the human has the last word.

issue, with leaders of HR, AI, and some aspects of operations. Front-line workers or (where they exist) unions should also be involved. The group should determine who will be impacted in what ways, how to prepare for the changes, and what organizational structures should be responsible for the transition.

We can't know exactly what will happen to the workforce as AI matures and proliferates, but it is very likely to become widely used within organizations. Many jobs and tasks will be affected by it. The earlier we begin preparing workers for this transition, the more likely they are to move successfully into a world of work that is augmented by smart machines.

A fully referenced version of this article is available from editor@dl-q.com

Tom Davenport *is a Distinguished Professor of Information Technology and Management at Babson College, a Fellow of the MIT Initiative on the Digital Economy, and a visiting professor at the UVA Darden School of Business.*

By Eve Psalti

Embracing AI in the Workplace

Balancing Technological Advancement with Human Collaboration

As artificial intelligence (AI) continues to evolve, it presents both opportunities and challenges for organizations. Harnessing AI's potential while preserving the collaborative and innovative spirit that is synonymous to human work necessitates a shift in both mindsets and organizational design. This delicate balance requires thoughtful integration of technology and a commitment to nurturing the unique qualities that we bring to the workplace.

A paramount shift that needs to happen first of all is around businesses and individuals adopting a growth mindset. Individuals need to embrace continuous learning and be open to evolving their skills. AI is a rapidly advancing field, and staying relevant requires a commitment to ongoing education and adaptability.

Creating an environment where we encourage experimentation can lead to breakthroughs in AI applications. Allowing employees to test new ideas without fear of failure promotes a culture of innovation and continuous improvement. Ethan Mollick, a Wharton associate professor, in his recent book called "Co-Intelligence – Living and Working with AI" explores AI can become an indispensable tool for many professionals. He worked with the Boston Consulting Group to run a study that found that the AI powered consultants (using popular Gen-AI tools) were faster in their assignments and their work was considered more creative, better written and more analytical. Mollick suggests to "always invite AI to the table, be the human in the loop and treat AI like an intelligent, yet inexperienced inter requiring instruction."

All AI solutions should be designed with the end-user in mind, ensuring they are intuitive and enhance the user experience. Involving employees in the design and implementation process can lead to more effective and user-friendly AI tools. As noted by Don Norman,

Creating an environment where we encourage experimentation can lead to breakthroughs in AI applications.

a pioneer in user-centered design, "We must design for the way people behave, not for how we would wish them to behave."

Furthermore, recognizing that change is a constant in the modern workplace can help reduce resistance and foster a more adaptable and resilient workforce. We should be creating a culture where employees view AI as a tool for enhancing their capabilities, not as a threat to their jobs. According to Satya Nadella, CEO of Microsoft, "Every person, organization, and even society as a whole can benefit from the digital transformation powered by AI." Investing in education and continuous learning programs to help workers acquire new skills relevant to the AI-driven job market.

Cultivating an understanding of how AI can complement human abilities is crucial. While many view AI as a competitor, I believe we can consider it as a collaborator that can handle repetitive tasks, allowing us to focus on creative and strategic activities.

As the AI models evolve, we will also need to consider the importance of ethics in AI deployment that ensures that technology is used responsibly.

As the AI models evolve, we will also need to consider the importance of ethics in AI deployment that ensures that technology is used responsibly. Organizations should establish guidelines for ethical AI use, considering implications for privacy, bias, and accountability.

Also, maintaining a human touch in interactions or as it's called "a human in the loop" especially in customer-facing roles, is essential. AI models can handle data analysis and pattern recognition, but empathy and emotional intelligence are uniquely human traits that enhance customer and employee experiences. As Sherry Turkle, MIT professor and author, points out, "We are at a moment when our technologies are seductive, but if we are not careful, we can be seduced in ways that diminish us."

Based on Marc Zao-Sanders'"How People Are Really Using GenAI" report for the Harvard Business Review that mined tens of thousands of posts in online forums like Redddit and Quora, researchers at Filtered found 100 kinds of applications of GenAI that feel into six broad categories. "As individuals and organizations experiment

with GenAI, use cases around these tools are proliferating... these include content creation and editing, technical assistance and troubleshooting, personal and professional support, learning and education, hobbies and recreation and research, analysis and decision-making."

Here are a couple of examples of businesses adopting AI to enhance their customer service, personalize customer experiences and develop new revenue streams.

Kroger, one of the largest grocery store chains in the United States, uses AI to improve customer experience and operational efficiency. Kroger leverages machine learning and AI services to provide personalized shopping experiences. The system analyzes customer purchase history and preferences to offer tailored product recommendations and promotions. AI services power Kroger's "smart shelves" that use digital displays and sensors to show real-time pricing and product information. These shelves can also detect when items are low in stock and alert store employees for replenishment.

Walgreens uses AI to provide better healthcare support through its virtual assistant. Walgreens' chatbot assists customers with healthcare-related queries, appointment scheduling, and prescription refills. The chatbot can handle common inquiries, freeing up pharmacists to focus on more complex tasks.

ASOS, a leading online fashion retailer, uses AI to enhance customer experiences and optimize operations. ASOS uses AI services, particularly computer vision, to enable visual search capabilities. Customers can upload photos of clothing items, and the AI matches these images with similar products available on the ASOS platform. Also, ASOS provides personalized product recommendations to customers based on their browsing history, preferences, and purchase behavior, enhancing the shopping experience.

TikTok wanted to enable users to connect and build community around shared topics. to transform the search experience to enable users to more efficiently connect users with content and creators that match their interests. So they launched a conversational bot, Tako, built on GenAI, which enables users to ask questions about content and creators on the platform that may be of interest. Through Tako, TikTok is enabling users to personalize their experience with and discovery of new content on the platform.

Financial institutions like American Express utilize AI to detect fraudulent transactions by analyzing patterns and anomalies in transaction data. This helps in preventing fraud and protecting customer accounts. Also, companies like ATCT and HP are using AI-powered chatbots and virtual assistants to handle customer inquiries, resolve issues, and provide support 24/7. These tools use natural language processing (NLP) to understand and respond to customer questions, reducing wait times and freeing up human agents for more complex tasks. Finally, healthcare providers are integrating AI to improve diagnostics and treatment plans. For example, AI can analyze medical images to detect diseases earlier and more accurately than traditional methods.

While the scenarios and use cases around AI integrations in the workplace will vary based on the industry, the geography and overall maturity of the AI capabilities, one thing is for sure: this integration should not come at the expense of the 'human magic' that drives creativity, collaboration, and innovation.

However, there are some common themes across organizations that have successfully integrated AI into their operations with positive results:

- They started with the business need and problem they needed to solve and then aligned the AI solution(s) to this strategy, not the other way around, adopting technology for its own sake. Leaders need to have a clear vision for how they want to transform or evolve their business and attach AI where it fits to drive efficiencies.

- They invest in skill development across the organization and foster a culture of innovation. As AI is rather new as a technology and rapidly evolving, it is important to increase AI literacy across teams and continue to upskill them along the way. Also,

AI integration should not come at the expense of the 'human magic' that drives creativity, collaboration, and innovation

creating a sandbox environment to encourage experimentation, adopt an agile mindset to fail fast, iterate and accelerate development is key. This practice is important also for establishing key performance indicators (KPIs) to measure success and ensure there is a

clear return on investment (ROI) from the AI technologies leveraged.

- They create an innovation gravity centre like a Centre of Excellence to foster collaboration across departments, bring diverse perspectives and share best practices across various disciplines. They also sponsor this effort with strong leadership involvement to ensure alignment across organizational goals.

By fostering the right mindsets and evolving organizational structures, businesses can harness the benefits of

"The entire point of embracing an AI transformation is to empower your people"

AI while maintaining the uniquely human qualities that lead to breakthroughs and meaningful work. As Daniela Rus, director of MIT's Computer Science and Artificial Intelligence Laboratory states in her recent book "The Mind's Mirror", "the entire point of embracing an AI transformation is to empower your people" going on to suggest that to best integrate AI into business operations we need to define a data plan, measure for bias and fairness, and develop a feedback loop to understand how employees are reacting to the new technology.

Ultimately, the goal is not to replace humans with machines but to create a synergistic environment where both can thrive. By doing so, organizations can leverage AI to enhance productivity and efficiency, while preserving the collaborative and innovative spirit that only humans can provide. This balanced approach will be key to thriving in the AI-driven future.

Eve Psalti is currently the Senior Director at Microsoft's Azure AI engineering organization responsible for scaling & commercializing AI solutions. Previously she was the Head of Strategic Platforms at Google Cloud. A native of Greece, Eve currently also serves on the board of WE Global Studios, a startup innovation studio supporting female entrepreneurs.

By Marcel Lukas

Leading in the Age of Generative AI

Challenges and Opportunities for Managers

The arrival of ChatGPT in November 2022 marked a watershed moment in the history of artificial intelligence. Within weeks, this generative AI tool had captured the imagination of millions, demonstrating an unprecedented ability to engage in human-like dialogue, generate creative content, and assist with complex problem-solving tasks. As we approach the end of 2024, it is clear that generative AI is not just another technological fad, but a transformative force that is reshaping the landscape of work across industries.

For leaders and managers, the rapid rise of generative AI presents both significant challenges and extraordinary opportunities. How can organizations harness the power of these tools to drive productivity and innovation? What new skills and strategies will leaders need to navigate this AI-augmented workplace? And how can we ensure that the integration of AI into our work processes is done in a way that is ethical, equitable, and aligned with human values?

This article explores these critical questions, drawing on recent research and real-world examples to provide a roadmap for leadership in the age of generative AI. As we will see, success in this new era requires not just technological savvy, but a fundamental rethinking of how we approach leadership, organizational culture, and the very nature of work itself.

The Current State of Generative AI Adoption

To understand the leadership implications of generative AI, we must first grasp the scale and speed of its adoption. A recent large-scale survey[1] conducted in Denmark provides a compelling snapshot of how quickly these tools are penetrating the workforce. Among workers

---

1   Humlum, Anders and Vestergaard, Emilie, The Adoption of ChatGPT. IZA Discussion Paper No. 16992, Available at SSRN: https://ssrn.com/abstract=4827166 or http://dx.doi.org/10.2139/ssrn.4827166

The rapid rise of generative AI presents both significant challenges and extraordinary opportunities. How can organizations harness the power of these tools to drive productivity and innovation?

in 11 occupations identified as particularly exposed to the potential impact of generative AI, a staggering 55% reported having used ChatGPT, with 40% having used it specifically for work purposes.

However, adoption rates vary significantly across professions. Software developers lead the pack, with 79% reporting use of ChatGPT, while financial advisors lag behind at 34%. This variance likely reflects differences in job requirements, organizational policies, and individual comfort with new technologies.

Early reports suggests that software development might be the 'killer app' for GenAI. One example was given by Amazon's CEO Andy Jassy who reported that Amazon saved 4,500 developer years by using AI for a software upgrade.

Interestingly, the study revealed several factors influencing adoption rates within professions. Younger and less experienced workers are more likely to use ChatGPT, with each additional year of age or experience associated with a 1.0 and 0.7 percentage point lower likelihood of using the tool, respectively. Workers with higher levels of education and better academic performance are also more likely to adopt generative AI tools.

Perhaps most strikingly, the study revealed a substantial gender gap in adoption. Women are about 20 percentage points less likely to use ChatGPT than men in the same occupation, even when controlling for factors like job specialization and task mix. This gender disparity has significant implications for workplace equity and the future of work, which we will explore in more detail later.

Younger and less experienced workers are more likely to use ChatGPT, with each additional year of age or experience associated with a lower likelihood of using the tool, respectively.

These adoption patterns suggest that while generative AI has the potential to be a great equalizer in the workplace, its benefits are not being distributed evenly across the workforce. This presents a critical challenge for leaders: how to ensure that all employees have the opportunity to benefit from these powerful new tools.

The Manager's Role in Shaping the Future of Work

As generative AI reshapes the workplace, managers find themselves at the forefront of a significant transition in how work is performed. The future of work will look markedly different, and managers play a crucial role not only in supporting their employees but also in creating the governance structures, IT infrastructure, and processes that allow for the safe and effective use of GenAI.

When an AI-employee can complete tasks in a fraction of the time it takes others, time-based evaluations become obsolete.

One of the key trends identified in Microsoft's future of work study is BYOAI (Bring Your Own AI), which presents both risks and opportunities for managers. On one hand, this trend increases the risk of data breaches, intellectual property violations, and other security concerns. Managers must be vigilant in establishing and enforcing clear policies around the use of personal AI tools in the workplace.

On the other hand, BYOAI can lead to significant productivity gains and innovation. Some employees may become what Ethan Mollick, an author and professor at the Wharton School who specializes in the impact of AI, terms "Hidden Cyborgs" – individuals who leverage AI tools to dramatically increase their output, potentially even reducing their working hours while maintaining or improving performance. This phenomenon presents a complex set of challenges for managers in today's AI-augmented workplace.

To safely realize the potential benefits of GenAI, organizations need to put the right support structures in place. Managers play a key role in this process by developing clear guidelines for AI use, ensuring proper data governance and security measures are in place, facilitating training programs to help employees use AI tools effectively and responsibly, and creating channels for employees to share best practices and innovations in AI use.

The rise of hidden cyborgs disrupts traditional performance evaluation methods. When an employee can complete tasks in a fraction of the time it takes others, time-based evaluations become obsolete. Managers must grapple with how to fairly assess and reward performance in a landscape where AI-assisted productivity varies widely among team members. This disparity can create equity issues, potentially leading to resentment if some team members are perceived as having an unfair advantage or if workload distribution becomes imbalanced.

Quality control emerges as another critical concern. While AI can significantly boost output quantity, managers need to ensure that the quality of work remains high. This requires developing new quality assurance processes that can keep pace with AI-enhanced productivity. Additionally, managers must be vigilant about the potential for over-reliance on AI tools. There is a risk

Share of survey respondents who are using AI tools at work not provided by their organization

Gen Z (18-28)	Millennials (18-28)	Gen X (44-57)	Boomers (58+)
85%	78%	76%	73%

Figure 1 Source: Microsoft Survey, 2024

that employees might become too dependent on AI assistance, potentially hindering the development of critical thinking and problem-solving skills that remain crucial in the workplace.

These shifts in productivity and work patterns also raise important questions about compensation and career progression. Should hidden cyborgs be compensated differently if they are significantly more productive? How does AI-enhanced performance factor into promotion decisions? Managers need to navigate these issues carefully to maintain a sense of fairness and motivation across their teams.

To address these challenges, managers must rethink their approach to performance evaluation, fostering a culture that values both AI-enhanced productivity and uniquely human skills. Open communication about AI use within teams becomes crucial, as does creating an environment where both AI-assisted and traditional work methods are respected and appropriately utilized.

To safely realize the potential benefits of GenAI while mitigating these risks, organizations need to put the right support structures in place. Managers play a key role in this process by developing clear guidelines for AI use, ensuring proper data governance and security measures are in place, facilitating training programs to help employees use AI tools effectively and responsibly, and creating channels for employees to share best practices and innovations in AI use.

Data governance in the context of AI use is particularly critical. It involves establishing comprehensive policies and procedures for how data is collected, stored, used, and shared when interacting with AI tools. A robust data governance framework should include a clear system for data classification, categorizing information based on its sensitivity and setting specific rules for how each category can be used with AI tools. For instance, highly sensitive customer data might be off-limits for use with external AI tools, while publicly available market data could be used more freely.

There is a risk that employees might become too dependent on AI assistance, potentially hindering the development of critical thinking and problem-solving skills.

Equally important is the implementation of strong data quality management processes. These ensure the accuracy, completeness, and reliability of data fed into AI systems through rigorous data cleaning, validation, and ongoing monitoring. Poor quality data can lead to inaccurate AI outputs, potentially resulting in flawed decision-making that could have far-reaching consequences for the organization.

Data access controls form another crucial component of effective AI governance. Managers need to work closely with IT teams to define and enforce policies about who can access what data and under what circumstances, especially when using external AI tools. This might involve implementing role-based access controls, multi-factor authentication, and detailed logging of data access to maintain security and compliance.

Perhaps most critically, managers must be acutely aware that existing data might contain biases from legacy observations of biased human decision-making. These biases could be related to race, gender, age, or

other protected characteristics. For example, historical hiring data might reflect past discriminatory practices, which could then be perpetuated or even amplified by AI systems trained on this data. Addressing this issue requires managers to work closely with data scientists and ethicists to identify and mitigate these biases, ensuring that AI tools don't inadvertently perpetuate or exacerbate existing inequalities.

By implementing these data governance measures alongside robust security protocols – such as encryption, API security, continuous monitoring, and data anonymization techniques – managers can help mitigate the risks associated with BYOAI while still harnessing its potential benefits. This balanced approach allows for innovation and productivity gains while protecting sensitive information, maintaining regulatory compliance, and striving for fairness and equity in AI-assisted decision-making.

As we navigate this new terrain, it is clear that the role of managers is evolving. They must become adept at balancing the opportunities presented by AI with the need to maintain a human-centered workplace. This requires not only technical knowledge but also heightened emotional intelligence, ethical decision-making skills, and the ability to guide their teams through rapid technological change. By rising to these challenges, managers can play a pivotal role in shaping a future of work that leverages the power of AI while preserving and enhancing the value of human contribution.

The significant gender gap in AI adoption revealed by the Danish study has important implications for managers. If we assume that GenAI improves productivity (which the study suggests it does), and that this improved productivity is rewarded accordingly, the higher use of GenAI by male workers could exacerbate existing gender income gaps. Managers must be proactive in addressing this disparity by encouraging and supporting women in using AI tools, ensuring equal access to AI training and resources, and regularly assessing and addressing any gender-based disparities in AI use and its impacts on performance evaluations and career progression.

Managers need to work closely with IT teams to define and enforce policies about who can access what data and under what circumstances

While companies with more male workers might currently face higher risks due to increased AI use, they may also be reaping more benefits in terms of productivity and innovation. Managers need to strike a delicate balance between encouraging AI adoption to drive productivity and innovation, and mitigating the associated risks. This balance can be achieved through regular risk assessments of AI use within the team or organization, implementing robust monitoring systems to detect potential misuse or security breaches, and fostering a culture of responsible AI use that values both innovation and security.

As AI tools enable employees to work more efficiently, managers may need to reassess traditional performance metrics and work structures. This could involve shifting focus from hours worked to outcomes achieved, implementing more flexible work arrangements that acknowledge AI-enhanced productivity, and developing new metrics that capture both quantitative output and qualitative factors like creativity, problem-solving, and strategic thinking.

Managers may need to reassess traditional performance metrics and work structures. This could involve shifting focus from hours worked to outcomes achieved

Managers must also grapple with the ethical implications of widespread AI use in the workplace. This includes issues of data privacy and consent when using AI tools, potential biases in AI outputs and how they might impact decision-making, transparency in AI use (particularly in customer-facing roles), and the impact of AI on job roles and potential displacement. Managers need to work closely with HR, legal teams, and ethics committees to develop guidelines that ensure AI is used in a way that aligns with the organization's values and ethical standards.

Leadership Opportunities with Generative AI

While the challenges are significant, generative AI also presents extraordinary opportunities for forward-thinking leaders to drive their organizations forward. One of the most significant opportunities lies in enhancing decision-making processes. By quickly analysing

vast amounts of data and generating insights, tools like ChatGPT can provide leaders with more comprehensive and nuanced information to inform their decisions. For instance, in fields like financial advising or marketing, AI can rapidly synthesize market trends, customer data, and economic indicators to provide more accurate forecasts and strategic recommendations. Leaders who effectively leverage these capabilities can make more informed, data-driven decisions at a pace that was previously impossible.

Another immediate benefit of generative AI is its ability to streamline routine tasks. The Danish study found that workers estimate ChatGPT can halve working times in about a third of their job tasks. This presents a significant opportunity for leaders to redesign workflows and reallocate human resources to higher-value

One of the most significant opportunities lies in enhancing decision-making processes

activities. For example, in customer service roles, AI can handle routine inquiries, freeing-up human agents to focus on more complex issues that require empathy and nuanced problem-solving. Similarly, in software development, AI can assist with routine coding tasks, allowing developers to focus on more creative and strategic aspects of their work.

Contrary to fears that AI might stifle human creativity, generative AI tools have the potential to enhance innovation by serving as powerful brainstorming partners and idea generators. Leaders can encourage their teams to use AI as a tool for exploring new possibilities and pushing the boundaries of what is possible. In fields like product design or marketing, AI can generate numerous creative concepts quickly, which human teams can then refine and develop. This human-AI collaboration can lead to more diverse and innovative solutions than either humans or AI might produce alone.

Perhaps most exciting is the potential for generative AI to enable entirely new business models and revenue streams. Forward-thinking leaders are already exploring how AI can be used to create personalized products and services at scale, enter new markets, or solve previously intractable problems. For instance, in the education sector, AI could enable highly personalized learning experiences tailored to each student's needs and learning style. In healthcare, AI could assist in developing personalized treatment plans based on a patient's genetic profile and medical history. Leaders who can identify and capitalize on these opportunities will be well-positioned to drive significant growth and value creation.

Conclusion: Embracing the Generative AI Revolution

As we have seen, the rise of generative AI presents both significant challenges and extraordinary opportunities for leaders and managers. Successfully navigating this new landscape will require a proactive approach that addresses the practical challenges of AI integration while also grappling with deeper questions about the changing nature of work, equity, and leadership.

Key imperatives for leaders in the age of generative AI include developing comprehensive AI strategies that align with organizational goals and values, creating robust governance structures and support systems for safe and effective AI use, addressing the gender gap in AI adoption to ensure equitable access to its benefits, balancing innovation and risk in the face of trends like

BYOAI, redefining performance metrics and work structures to reflect AI-enhanced productivity, and ensuring ethical and responsible AI use across the organization.

The leaders who can successfully navigate these challenges will be well-positioned to drive their organizations to new heights of productivity, innovation, and success. As we move deeper into the age of generative AI, it is clear that the most effective leaders will be those who can harness the power of AI while also amplifying the uniquely human qualities that no machine can replicate.

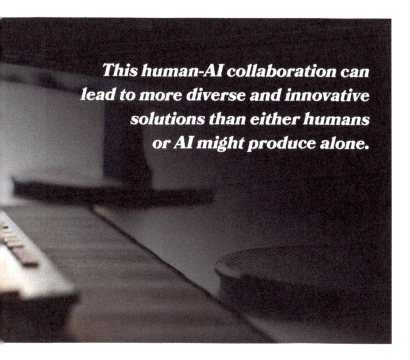

This human-AI collaboration can lead to more diverse and innovative solutions than either humans or AI might produce alone.

The generative AI revolution is here, and it is transforming the world of work at an unprecedented pace. By embracing this change and proactively addressing its implications, leaders can shape a future where human potential is augmented and amplified by AI, creating organizations that are more innovative, productive, and ultimately, more equitable and human.

Dr Marcel Lukas *is a Senior Lecturer in Banking & Finance and Director of Executive Education at the University of St Andrews. His research interest focuses on the influence of technology on financial decision making and leadership.*

By Rimma Boshernitsan

The Triad of Intelligences

Harnessing Machine, Planetary, and Human Intuition in the Age of AI

A I is not just a technological advancement; it's a catalyst that is transforming the way humans are relating to themselves and the world around them.

As we rush to embrace this new frontier—one that promises the productivity boost we have been waiting for—we might want to consider our access to the multitude of intelligences that exist around us and our abilities to synthesize their impact on how we perceive ourselves, our contexts, and our world at large. Could creating a *co-intelligent* approach be the resolve we are all seeking?

We should not forget that we have three super-intelligences at our fingertips—machine intelligence, planetary intelligence, and human intelligence—which together form a cohesive framework that guides our decisions and actions

Perhaps. Yet in navigating the complexity of this landscape, we should not forget that we have three super-intelligences at our fingertips—machine intelligence, planetary intelligence, and human intelligence—which together form a cohesive framework that guides our decisions and actions at work, at home, and beyond.

Machine Intelligence: The Rise of AI

First, let's talk about machine intelligence. Embodied by AI, it has quickly become a defining feature of the 21st century. From automating routine tasks to predicting complex patterns, AI is reshaping industries and redefining the possibilities of human achievement. Yet, although AI's capabilities are impressive, they are not without limitations.

At its core, machine intelligence is about processing vast amounts of data and generating outcomes based on patterns and algorithms. AI excels at tasks that require speed, precision, and the ability for analysis far beyond human capacity. In industries such as finance, health care, and logistics, AI has already demonstrated its potential to streamline operations, reduce errors, and unlock new efficiencies and opportunities.

However, AI's strengths also highlight its weaknesses. Machine intelligence is inherently linear and lacks the ability to understand context, nuance, or emotion. Artist and longtime critic of AI, Trevor Paglen has highlighted

how these systems often operate within opaque infra-structures, raising concerns about transparency and accountability. In effect machine intelligence does not sense nor does it sense-make. It *can* process data, but it cannot interpret the deeper meanings and contexts that often drive human decision-making. AI operates within the boundaries of its programming, making it susceptible to biases embedded in the data it processes. Nuance is still largely lost on AI and it is this limitation in particular that affects outcomes when it is used for decision-making processes that impact human lives, as in hiring, law enforcement, and medical diagnoses.

Unlike human or machine logic, planetary intelligence operates through a web of relationships, feedback loops, and emergent phenomena—all principles that can inspire more resilient and adaptive business strategies.

The role of machine intelligence in our future is not yet clear—but we know that it is a powerful tool that can augment human capabilities and drive the speed of innovation. Yet as we integrate AI into our organizations and societies, we must do so within a co-intelligent framework that understands its foibles and vulnerabilities. AI should serve as an enabler, not a replacement, of human intelligence.

Planetary Intelligence: Tapping in to the Wisdom of Nature

While machine intelligence occupies the forefront of technology, planetary intelligence reminds us of the timeless wisdom embedded in the natural world. Planetary intelligence comprises the interconnectedness of ecosystems, the delicate balance of natural processes, and the organic knowledge that has evolved over millennia. Unlike human or machine logic, planetary intelligence operates through a web of relationships, feedback loops, and emergent phenomena—all principles that can inspire more resilient and adaptive business strategies. What would it mean to look beyond our conventional frameworks in order to seek answers that reshape our perceptions? As leaders, we are often faced with binary decision-making processes—if this, then that. When complexity arises, we tend to revert to what we know, to stay where our intellect is most comfortable. But what if we could expand our understanding through lenses we usually overlook?

Marshall McLuhan's idea that "the medium is the message" prompts us to reflect on how our tools—such as AI—shape our understanding of the world. Integrating the wisdom of nature into our strategies can lead to more holistic and sustainable approaches. Our ability to distill insights from diverse inputs, particularly those from the natural world, is not just an intellectual exercise; it is a strategic advantage that can transform business outcomes and deepen our connections to the markets we serve.

Consider Japan's Shinkansen Bullet Train as an example of aligning technology with planetary intelligence. Faced with the challenge of reducing noise from sonic booms, engineers looked to nature for inspiration. They studied the kingfisher, known for its ability to dive into water with minimal splash due to its uniquely shaped beak. Mimicking the bird's form, they reshaped the train's nose, significantly reducing noise while increasing speed and energy efficiency. How could we envision more imaginative, ethical uses of technology—those that are effective and respectful of the planet's needs?

This case study highlights how aligning with planetary intelligence, using biomimicry to learn from a process in nature, and looking beyond human or machine logic can lead to more intentionally designed solutions. Nature's solutions, honed over aeons, are often more efficient, sustainable, and insightful than human-engineered alternatives. By integrating these insights into our strategies, we can solve immediate challenges while creating technologies and systems that harmonize with the natural world, enhancing business performance and rewarding environmental stewardship.

Human Intelligence and Intuition: The Unique Human Aspect

We can harness machine intelligence and even the wisdom of planetary intelligence, but we must not overlook our unique ability to intuit—to use our all-too-human intelligence to assess our contexts and act accordingly.

To fully leverage human intuition, we must cultivate it as a skill. This means creating environments that encourage reflection, mindfulness, and the convergence of various perspectives

Human intuition is the ability to understand something instinctively, without conscious reasoning. It is the culmination of our experiences, our emotions, and the subtle cues we pick up from the world around us. It is that gut feeling we all know.

For some, intuition comes naturally; for others, it is less familiar. In leadership, it is often seen as unquantifiable and is therefore undervalued. McLuhan's theories suggest that technology shapes our sensory perceptions, but intuition enables us to navigate complexity and ambiguity. In leadership, intuition helps us make decisions that are beyond the data, anticipate trends based on our sense-making abilities and our past experiences, and relate to everything around us.

We now know that the heart and brain communicate, influencing each other's function. The heart sends signals to the brain that can affect emotional processing, decision-making, and overall well-being. So, to fully leverage human intuition, we must cultivate it as a skill. This means creating environments that encourage reflection, mindfulness, and the convergence of various perspectives. It also means recognizing intuition's value in decision-making and giving it equal weight alongside data and analysis.

In his book, *Wild Problems*, Russ Roberts talks about Charles Darwin's significant personal dilemma:

Some of life's most important decisions can't be reduced to a simple cost-benefit analysis. Instead, they require to be guided by one's intuition, values, and a willingness to embrace uncertainty

whether or not to marry. Darwin, known for his scientific rigour and analytical mind, approached this decision in a methodical way, listing out the pros and cons of marriage. Roberts uses Darwin's decision-making process as an example of how even the most rational and logical thinkers struggle with decisions that have no clear, calculable answer—what Roberts refers to as „wild problems." These are the types of problems that don't have a definitive right or wrong answer and often involve weighing intangible factors like happiness, fulfillment, and personal values.

Roberts uses this example to also argue that some of life's most important decisions can't be reduced to a simple cost-benefit analysis. Instead, they require to be guided by one's intuition, values, and a willingness to embrace uncertainty. What could Darwin's decision-making process look like if he approached it with co-intelligence in mind?

Co-Intelligence: The Interplay of the Three Intelligences

The future will not be shaped by machine intelligence, planetary intelligence, or human intuition alone. Instead, it will be defined by the interplay among these three super-intelligences, each contributing its unique strengths to create a more balanced and holistic approach to problem-solving.

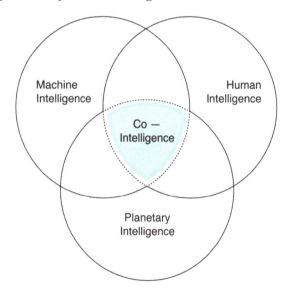

In practical terms, this means integrating these intelligences into the fabrics of our organizations, communities, and societies. For example, AI can predict natural

It is up to us to consciously design systems and processes that facilitate co-intelligence—the collaboration among machine intelligence, planetary intelligence, and human intuition

disasters, but it is human intuition that is required to mobilize communities and coordinate responses. Planetary intelligence guides our understanding of ecosystems, AI helps optimize resource use, and human intuition drives ethical decision-making.

The synergy among these intelligences suggests profound implications for creating new inventions, products, and ways of enhancing our relationship with technology. By combining AI's analytical power, planetary intelligence's sustainability principles, and human intuition's creativity, we can develop solutions that are not only effective but also ethical and sustainable.

However, achieving this synergy requires a conscious effort. It is up to us to consciously design systems and processes that facilitate *co-intelligence—* the collaboration among machine intelligence, planetary intelligence, and human intuition. This includes developing AI technologies that are transparent and explainable, promoting cross-disciplinary learning that bridges the gap between technology and nature, and fostering cultures that value both data and intuition.

Ethical Implications and Future Considerations

As with any technology, integrating these three intelligences raises ethical questions. AI's potential to disrupt industries, economies, and societies is enormous, and we must ensure these disruptions don't come at the cost of human dignity or environmental sustainability.

One key ethical challenge is the potential for AI to exacerbate existing inequalities and biases. As AI becomes more embedded in decision-making, those who control it may gain disproportionate power. What would it mean to include fairness, transparency, and accountability as part of the governance processes that we create?

The rapid pace of technological development often outstrips our ability to fully understand its consequences.

Another ethical consideration is the need to preserve the integrity of human intuition. We are creating a world where AI can increasingly mimic human behaviour, and for this reason we have to not only be careful not to lose sight of the unique qualities that make us human, but also to create parameters that keep aware of the context of the technologies we use. What would it mean to consciously set up ways of keeping ourselves and our technologies "in check"? How could we begin to value empathy, creativity, and ethical reasoning as much as we value data and efficiency?

Lastly, consider the long-term impact of AI on the planet. The rapid pace of technological development often outstrips our ability to fully understand its consequences. As stewards of both technology and the environment, our responsibility is to ensure that AI is developed in a way that supports the health and resilience of the planet.

As we move forward into the age of AI, we stand at a crossroads. We have the opportunity to harness the power of machine intelligence, the wisdom of planetary intelligence, and the unique insights of human intuition to create a future that is not only innovative but also ethical and sustainable, but this future will not happen by itself. It requires a conscious effort to integrate these three intelligences into our decision-making processes, our organizational cultures, and our societal structures. It requires us to ask difficult questions, challenge our assumptions, and embrace the complexity of the world around us.

By doing so, we can ensure that AI serves as a tool for human flourishing, that our technological advancements are aligned with the needs of the planet, and that our intuition remains a guiding force in the decisions that shape our future.

In this new era, the balance of machine intelligence, planetary intelligence, and human intuition is not just a possibility—it is a necessity. The choices we make today will determine the world we leave for future generations. Let us choose wisely.

Rimma Boshernitsan is a futurist, a strategist and the CEO of DIALOGUE, an interdisciplinary strategic advisory with a focus on cross-sector, human connected transformation and intelligent innovation. She also serves as a fellow at the Center for the Future of Organization.

By George Barnett

You May be More Ready for Generative AI Than You Think

O ver the past year of generative AI break-throughs, most people have been talking about use cases that are not that much different from what machine learning offered – automation, productivity, recruiting, acceler-ated methods of classification, prediction and natural language processing.

What they are not talking about is how generative AI will play an outsized role in strategy development – both at the corporate level as well as at the functional, business unit, product and brand levels. And how the all-important "first mover advantage" will deliver supe-rior returns to those who act now.

The high costs of generative AI software development and the intense war for AI talent are raising new barriers to competitive entry for even the fastest of fast followers

I hear this complaint time and time again. A group of middle managers, over drinks, comparing their first attempts to get something out of this innovation. The one who gets the most laughs used it to generate top ten lists for travel. Not exactly earth-shattering stuff.

As many have already observed, there are tiny, incremental improvements in productivity that each of us can eek out of these first-generation tools. Nudges to help us think more broadly, use more comprehensive spell-checking, translation and, yes, search. However, beyond the immediate gains experienced by die-hard software coders and brand marketing professionals, there is a dearth of useful use cases out there.

This lack of great use cases may lead to cynicism, but what we witness are just the same adoption dynamics as in previous waves of software innovation (think about the first spreadsheets, word processors, and graphics tools). Over time, most people will experiment with these generative AI tools in the course of their daily work, until better versions, more applied versions, come along. And they learn in the process.

Companies that are Bypassing the Hype Curve

There are a few market leaders that have already gone past this phase. They are going beyond "hopping on the hype curve".

Adobe is a prime example. Rather than wait for newcomers Midjourney or Stable Diffusion to disrupt their hold on the creativity marketplace, Adobe created and rolled out their own version of generative AI for visuals, called Firefly, to much acclaim. Firefly not only works simply and easily within designers' workflows, but it also deftly avoids any potential legal issues by not being trained on the unauthorized intellectual property of others.

Another example is **Accenture**, who announced that it will invest up to $3B to train an army of their employees to be AI-focused, both in order to use generative AI more in its client work, as well as support those customers in their use of the technology. All on the heels of similar press releases from PwC, EY, Bain, Deloitte, IBM, BCG, and McKinsey, who has already rolled out a ChatGPT-like bot called Lilli.

And big tech has taken note, of course, as it faces potential disruption.

Alphabet is on 'code red' to protect its core search engine business, trying to offer all the excitement of the new technology to users that opt-in, without taking the unnecessary risk of upsetting the status quo. Through this "labs approach", including partnering with new players such as Anthropic, and systemically rolling out Gemini, Alphabet plays to its strengths as a data giant, gathering a flywheel of user information to improve its foundational models and applications.

Microsoft, on the other hand, with OpenAI and ChatGPT in its back pocket, sees only an upside in dominating the narrative of being an innovator again. It is using its massive distribution advantage and installed base of enterprise customers to keep pushing the boundaries of when, where and how a person develops the habit of relying on one of its software "co-pilots" or agents to get work done.

Even **Apple** is rethinking its strategy, announcing the release of its model, Ajax, and its chatbot (and Siri replacement) codenamed Apple GPT, in conjunction with its new iPhone 16 line-up.

What are the implications for the vast majority of companies who are faced with the above-mentioned conundrum?

New technology like generative AI does not change the fundamental questions but has a lot to do with how to answer them

Opportunities Abound...

In times of uncertainty and disruptive change, it makes sense to go back to basics. Corporate strategy means making clear choices about what to do and what not to do as a business. Corporate strategy looks at capabilities that competitors don't have or would struggle to have and, based on these insights, targets markets and shapes its products and services accordingly. New technology like generative AI does not change the fundamental questions but has a lot to do with how to answer them. It is important to recognize that generative AI tools are simply the latest innovation in a company's enterprise software "stack". And, just as with their existing software, companies can take advantage of these new generative AI tools to refresh and stress-test their corporate strategy.

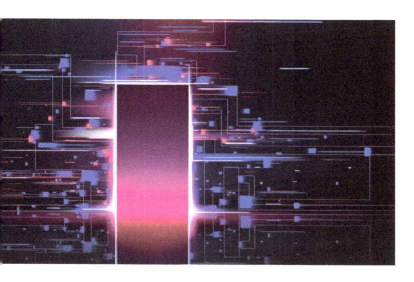

Take for example brainstorming – a key practice when it comes to developing novel strategic ideas. GenAI is radically changing the game here. Not unlike scientific researchers in the life sciences, companies can set up a literature-based discovery (LBD) process to look for hypotheses, connections or ideas that humans may have missed. They can expand their training datasets to include every idea they ever considered, those chosen and those rejected, along with the rationale. It is possible to create a proprietary chatbot trained on this internal dataset and query away. Companies can apply tests that allow them to challenge assumptions. They can broaden their constraints with externally acquired datasets from a diverse range of sources. Experiment with "how to win" dimensions such as the degree of autonomy, ranging

A new AI strategy will result in new data to be used as input to the next cycle of strategy formation.

from fully autonomous to human-in-the-loop. Add more data. Iterate, iterate, iterate. These are leapfrog opportunities for a creative strategy process.

Existing analytical tools are about to change dramatically, too, as they present an interface layer that is intelligent and driven by underlying algorithms. Companies like Microsoft, Alphabet, Salesforce, and Adobe are offering their next generation of office productivity software – spreadsheets, data mining, visualization, observability, design tools, CRMs, and more – accelerating turnaround times on each task and query. Companies will need a team of analysts able to maximize the value of these new applications, working alongside traditional strategists. If they manage to do this well, they will gain a competitive advantage.

Lastly, an exciting feature of corporate strategy in a time of generative AI is that, properly designed and executed, a new AI strategy will result in new data to be used as input to the next cycle of strategy formation. In other words, we may see the start of a more dynamic system of strategy-in-use.

Capitalizing on Internal Data

Much has been written about the 'rough and ready' nature of the outputs of Generative AI. They have even coined the phrase 'hallucinate' to describe the errors introduced by the software. It is a classic case of GIGO (garbage in, garbage out). You need to know the source

datasets used for training the algorithms and for building the LLMs (large language models) in order to determine the quality of the output. To use GenAI effectively, it is important to apply your existing know-how in identifying and mitigating biases and errors before your customers do; you must pay special attention to inputs, models, and algorithms.

To use GenAI effectively, it is important to apply your existing know-how in identifying and mitigating biases and errors before your customers do.

Given the complexity and 'black box' nature of the new tools, strategists and executives need the support of AI specialists capable of explaining the underlying rationale for which AI generated option rises to the top (which requires expert knowledge of the input datasets and tools used), and what the tradeoffs are by not going with the second or third placed option.

Equally important is the issue of relevance, or specificity. Depending on a company's strategic goals, there will be preferences and priorities as to which datasets should be used. Companies may even want to include their proprietary datasets, especially custom data that grow and refresh over time.

Models get stronger if they are fed a company's entire history of internal documentation, across functions, along with financials, communications, product performance, etc. No longer are there data-related limits to what can be incorporated in the models. As Adrian Cockcroft of OrionX.net stated, "You're fine-tuning the model to be somebody that understands your company."

There are many different ways to marry external AI tools with internal data so that ChatGPT can then generate responses customized to a company's unique circumstances. One option is to fine-tune the GenAI engine against proprietary datasets, which requires in-house expertise in API access and in the use of software libraries such as TensorFlow or PyTorch to do the heavy lifting of the training process. Or you may choose to refine your prompt engineering methods against your own database, and then use those custom-tailored prompts to query the external engine. However, both options present trade-offs in terms of accuracy and expense.

A Back-to-Basics Game Plan

To take advantage of these opportunities, it is important to candidly assess your capabilities and make a 'buy' versus 'build' decision. Large-scale digital natives such as Amazon or Microsoft enjoy a very different talent and capability situation as industrial legacy players. Depending on the various contexts, companies will have to choose their distinctive AI strategy. How much should they leverage external tools and data, how much can or should they develop inside to best capitalize on their internal data sets? Is it better to create an own in-house LLM or fine-tune an open-source LLM on their own data?

The answer is it depends, as both approaches have their pros and cons: In-house LLMs offer the advantages of full data ownership, more control, and lower cost of inference (the cost of asking the LLM to generate a response), but deliver lower performance along with greater risk and cost of safety.

APIs (application programming interfaces that connect with external solutions) are the mirror-image; they offer the advantages of higher performance along with the ability to offload risk and cost of safety, but require the sharing of data, resulting in less control, and in a higher cost of inference.

While the trade-offs are clear, the costs and complexities are significant. If your company is among the fortunate few that have the abilities and resources, you may have already built or are building a contender. Most companies are not that lucky; and just like with any new category of enterprise software, they need to choose between experimenting and the available commercial options.

Capitalizing on these opportunities requires more than just investments in technology. It requires talent that is not only AI-savvy but also has the domain expertise and experience to assess if these words and numbers that are generated by the new tools make sense.

One executive described how they use multiple suppliers, how each is slightly different, and how each generates content that is beneficial for different use cases. By embracing this diversity, they are building in-house proprietary expertise in how to use each piece of the puzzle to its maximum potential.

If these issues sound familiar, it is because they are. We have seen the same dynamic in cloud-computing, when companies debate about proprietary versus hosted solutions.

A New Set of Capabilities

It is evident that each step of the corporate strategy process – from picking markets and products to deploying capital and capabilities – can benefit from incorporating generative AI tools. But capitalizing on these opportunities requires more than just investments in technology. It requires talent that is not only AI-savvy but also has the domain expertise and experience to assess if these words and numbers that are generated by the new tools make sense.

In this context, it is important to revisit the assessment of a company's capabilities. What are the pre-existing and/or nascent skills and resources critical to the use of generative AI? What must be developed or sourced from outside experts? Be brutally honest as to what your company can and cannot do, and what it may take to address any gaps.

So yes, corporate strategy changes in a time of generative AI. What the internal team of strategists does changes. What external consultants do changes. The capabilities needed to succeed change, and so do the needs for collaboration in the AI-related ecosystem. What probably won't change are the investments in strategy. Like the waves of automation and robotics in the past, the advent of generative AI itself does not threaten you or your company. It is the sophisticated use of generative AI by your competitors that is the threat.

George Barnett is a strategy consultant with the CapSys Group, having held leadership roles at the ClearLake Group and the Monitor Group. He specializes in technology and corporate strategy and is the author of the leading Substack newsletter The Strategy Toolkit, *and the book* Know Your Capabilities.

By Roy Tomizawa

From Indecision to Action

How Executive Education Can Help Leaders Navigate the Shift to AI

Large Language Models. Retrieval Augmented Generation. Computer Vision. Generative AI. Prompt Engineering. Maybe you know those words. Most people don't. But with the advent of the popular ChatGPT chatbot and the incredible pace of advancement in the field of artificial intelligence, those words are becoming essential vocabulary for leaders of organizations large and small.

"The challenge is we're now in a cycle where things are moving exponentially. So just doing a discrete session of business transformation isn't enough because by the time you finish, you're already behind again."

And for all the so-called "hallucinations" of chatbots like Gemini or Claude or ChatGPT that we hear about, AI expert Ian Beacraft said that these models are improving at the extraordinary rate of 5 to 10 times per year, which is problematic for leaders.

"The challenge," Beacraft said during his SXSW 2024 presentation, "is we're now in a cycle where things are moving exponentially. So just doing a discrete session of business transformation isn't enough because by the time you finish, you're already behind again. We're now in an era where regeneration, constant regeneration is necessary, not just one moment of transformation."

As a result, leaders are bewildered by this hyper-change. According to a recent BCG study, 66% of executives surveyed are "ambivalent or outright dissatisfied with their organization's progress on AI and generative AI so far."

Some are taking action, but most are still in consideration mode. The same survey showed that 90% of executives surveyed are "either waiting for GenAI to move beyond the hype or experimenting in small ways." That report suggests that these companies are "observers… opting for a wait-and-see approach. That's not an option with generative AI."

Why are so many leaders stuck in analysis paralysis? To be fair, caution is a common human response in the face of such sudden change and uncertainty. According to this 2024 survey of leaders and machine learning experts, there are many reasons why AI is not the number one focus of many organizations.

Why AI Not Adopted Yet	%
1. Security/data concerns	28%
2. Lack of expertise	26%
3. Other initiatives take priority	22%
4. Waiting for AI tech to mature	21%
5. Lack of budget	18%
6. Traditional tech meets needs	15%
7. No applicable use case	13%
8. No executive support	11%
9. Don't know	5%

Source: Scale.com's AI Readiness Report 2024 Zeitgeist

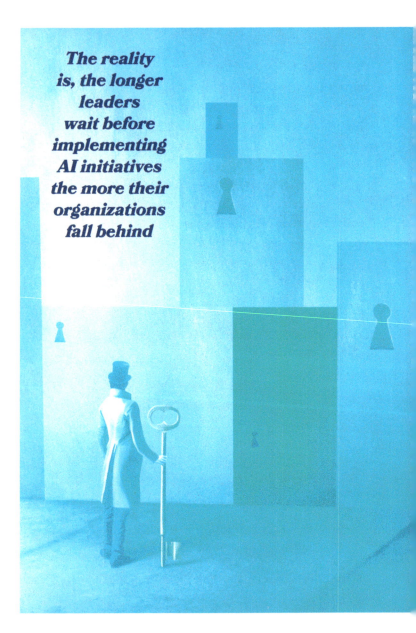

The reality is, the longer leaders wait before implementing AI initiatives the more their organizations fall behind

Leaders often cite legitimate concerns, for example, of employees pasting sensitive and confidential data into a chatbot, or the lack of AI expertise in their organizations, or the fact that their current processes are more of a match for their traditional tech, and would not align easily to AI systems. They need more time to understand AI and how to implement it safely and effectively, they say.

But the reality is, the longer leaders wait, the more their organizations fall behind. Leaders know what BCG has uncovered in its 2024 survey of over 1,400 executives: they have a "lack of AI talent and skills," an "unclear AI and GenAi roadmap and investment priorities," and have "no strategy for responsible AI and Gen AI."

And many are genuinely worried because not only is their organizational AI acumen low, nearly 60% of leaders surveyed by BCG say they have limited or no confidence in their executive team's proficiency in GenAI. This is a shame because it isn't all that expensive or difficult to implement AI tools or processes.

It is certainly easy and inexpensive to learn quickly. Leaders need to make time to read, watch and participate in the ample books, articles, videos, online courses, conferences and face-to-face training courses available.

University executive education also has a huge role to play here. There are three powerful ways to leverage executive education to drive AI activation in organizations:

Leaders need to understand how AI is being applied today, to reflect on how AI can impact their company direction and strategy.

- **Create Time for Leaders to Understand, Reflect and Plan:** Leaders need time to reflect on how to handle this period of uncertainty. Leaders need to understand how AI is being applied today, to reflect on how AI can impact their company direction and strategy, as well as to reflect on the ways to break through the walls of uncertainty and take decisive action. Leaders also need time to know when AI is not the answer, that design of effective processes before or instead of AI implementation is a greater need. Many university flagship leadership programs put AI front and centre in a curriculum designed to slow down one's thinking in consideration of what it takes to go from current to desired state, when and when not to apply AI.

- **Accelerate Development and Performance of Hi-Pos:** Leaders need to leverage their high-performers, who are commonly their AI champions and driving higher EBIT than the rest of the organization, according to a 2022 McKinsey report. This is an opportunity for leaders to work with an external providers to design a hi-po-leadership development program that leverages their extant AI acumen to focus on the company's thorniest issues or strategic initiatives.

- **Build Organizational AI Literacy:** Many organizations have discouraged employees from using AI tools due to concerns about data and privacy. Measures need to be taken so that organizations do not force employees to use GenAI in the shadows, and keep their tips and tricks a secret. In fact, you want to grow AI literacy throughout the organization. In order to leverage the most generally available AI tool, the large language model, providing training in critical thinking skills can go a long way in leveraging the true analytical and creative powers of these chatbots.

Roy Tomizawa is Chief Executive of Sasin Executive Education. Roy has worked in Singapore, the US, and Japan, and held senior HR leadership positions for Mercer, Morgan Stanley, Microsoft, DBS Bank, Nikko Asset Management, and MetLife Insurance. Roy is also the author of two books on Thailand: Working with the Thais *and* Start Up and Stay Up in Thailand*; and one about Japan:* 1964: The Greatest Year in the History of Japan.

By Abigail Kramer

The Age of AI and the Need for More Humane Leadership

On September 12, 2024, Oprah Winfrey hosted a prime-time television special on AI, featuring Sam Altman, Bill Gates, and other prominent figures. Nothing captures the zeitgeist quite like a television special with Oprah, which tends to draw an audience of 10-15 million viewers.

The launch of ChatGPT 3.5 in November 2022 marked the dawn of the Age of AI. Since then, the industry has dominated headlines. Tech giants have poured billions into securing their place at the forefront, while companies across every sector are exploring AI to unlock breakthrough productivity gains. Meanwhile, policymakers scramble to provide the necessary guardrails, and tens of thousands of startups are flooding the market with AI-driven solutions.

In this context, Samudra members have come together to explore the potential impact of generative AI on organizations and communities. Samudra is an "ecosystem of communities of purpose" where leaders from diverse backgrounds collaborate to address complex, intersectional challenges. Participants include board members, CEOs, business and technology executives, as well as thought leaders from various disciplines.

Below is a summary of the key insights from recent discussions. Samudra operates under "Chatham House Rules," which does not allow perspectives and statements to be attributed to individual members. However, we are happy to share some high-level insights based on conversations and qualitative research:

1. AI investments will continue despite the "trough of disillusionment."

Even as we go through market disillusionment and pullback, investments in AI will persist for years due to several driving factors: (1) the unwillingness of tech giants to relinquish market dominance to competitors, (2) the continued interest from companies who see benefits by deploying AI, and (3) the potential for a

As generative AI becomes more accessible to consumers and integrates into devices like smartphones, we can expect an explosion of new applications and use cases.

global AI arms race – especially between China and the US – compelling governments to aggressively pursue this technology.

The nature of AI investments will evolve, with rapid and often unpredictable shifts. For example, venture capital has already moved quickly from investing in AI infrastructure to AI applications, and now to AI "agents." As generative AI becomes more accessible to consumers and integrates into devices like smartphones, we can expect an explosion of new applications and use cases.

Fundamentally, generative AI is seen as a foundational platform shift —similar to the transformative impact of mobile phones and the Internet— with the potential to create deep, widespread changes across all industries and sectors of society. As such, significant investments in this space will continue.

The bigger, unaddressed question is whether current governance structures are sufficient. We cannot rely on public policy to keep pace, even if our governments are willing to regulate AI.

2.   Proper AI governance is a major concern at the top

In a recent poll among Samudra board members, AI emerged as one of three top priorities, with special emphasis on associated risks and governance. For example, there is concern about the potential liabilities companies could face if AI delivers a faulty response to a patient or causes financial harm to a customer.

The bigger, unaddressed question is whether current governance structures are sufficient. We cannot rely on public policy to keep pace, even if our governments are willing to regulate AI. Moreover, most corporate governance frameworks are not designed for such rapid change. There is a clear need to tightly integrate informed governance with product and service development and delivery.

3. *Many organizations are assembling internal platforms to develop AI-powered applications.*

Companies are leveraging AI for business value in three main ways. The first is partnering directly with AI providers (e.g., OpenAI, Nvidia) to develop proprietary large language models (LLMs) for competitive advantage. This high-risk, high-reward strategy is feasible only for companies with deep financial resources and access to rare technical talent.

The second approach is to leverage the AI capabilities that come bundled with various cloud software providers. This is relatively easy to implement and can quickly offer limited productivity gains (e.g., instant document summaries, meeting transcripts, etc.), but experience shows that

the costs are still too high compared to the value. Worse still, these gains fail to differentiate the business, as any company can subscribe to the same services.

The third option is assembling an internal platform that applies external LLMs to proprietary corporate data to create business-specific applications that provide a competitive edge. We see more organizations adopting this approach, with some vendors offering ready-made platforms to accelerate this process rather than building from scratch.

This presents an opportunity for companies to join ecosystems where they can pool data for mutual benefit or to form partnerships where they exchange their data for AI expertise and development.

4. Data management with unstructured data will be essential for deriving value.

The technology leaders within Samudra —such as Chief Information, Data, and Digital Officers— consistently emphasize that they must manage and govern their unstructured data correctly in order to capitalize on the promise of AI. They refer to the entirety of documents and content assets in an organization – spreadsheets, images, videos, contracts, architecture diagrams, formulas, project plans, resumes, customer feedback, and chats, just to name a few.

However, not all unstructured data hold value for the business. The challenge is identifying which data are unique and valuable to the company and then using AI to capitalize on that.

A corresponding insight is that not every organization has access to the volume and diversity of proprietary data necessary to gain a competitive edge. This presents an opportunity for companies to join ecosystems where they can pool data for mutual benefit or to form partnerships where they exchange their data for AI expertise and development.

5. ROI will hinge on enabling multiple, differentiating use cases over time.

Just as the Internet and mobile technology have transformed how we work and live our lives, we believe that the return on investment from AI will stem from enabling multiple use cases over time. This requires building a flexible AI-enabled technology platform to support multiple flavors of LLMs, AI applications, emerging devices, and more.

The best place to start is to identify what business challenges, customer needs, or new capabilities will benefit the organization most. In other words, don't start with the technology; start with the business case. With this in mind, many organizations have established cross-functional "AI Governance Councils" with representatives from various departments (including legal, HR, finance, IT and the business) to collectively assess opportunities, manage risks, and guide AI initiatives.

Meanwhile, various vendors and startups are working hard to develop AI-based applications tailored to specific industries and use cases. Some examples include contract review for the legal industry, fraud detection in financial services, and creating voice-over videos in marketing.

6. *Consider that Generative AI has emerging "superpowers" that you can leverage at scale.*

While we consider business-differentiating use cases, it's helpful to think of generative AI as having distinct "superpowers" we're discovering over time. For example:

- Finding Information: AI can revolutionize search functions by quickly retrieving and synthesizing relevant data, potentially disrupting traditional search engines.
- Analyzing Information: AI can summarize content, answer questions about documents, and perform other analytical tasks, enhancing our ability to process and understand information.
- Creating Information: AI can generate a wide range of content, including images, videos, text, and code, enabling new forms of creative and technical expression.
- Performing Tasks: AI-driven automation and intelligent agents can handle repetitive tasks, streamline workflows, and support various business processes.
- Helping People: AI can assist with training, learning, and even coaching, providing personalized support and enhancing human development.

AI clearly has the potential to displace workers, possibly eliminating entire job families.

These superpowers become even more impressive when applied at scale. Analyzing a single document is relatively simple, but analyzing 1,000 legal documents simultaneously is a significant challenge. Similarly, generating a few images is one thing, but producing hundreds of "good enough" images quickly —ones that your creative team can refine into final products— is another level of capability and value.

7.   Change management and adoption will be essential for realizing value.

As with any technology, adoption and effective use are crucial for success. AI presents unique challenges in driving change and increasing utilization within organizations.

AI clearly has the potential to displace workers, possibly eliminating entire job families. We're already seeing early signals where businesses let go of lower-performing employees to offset the high costs associated with implementing AI, or reduce hiring for open positions, expecting AI to boost productivity.

This puts significant structural and cultural change pressure on companies. Depending on how this change is managed, employees may perceive AI as a threat or an ally, which can accelerate or inhibit adoption and value. At any rate, the impact of AI on the workplace environment will be massive, politically charged, and will challenge leaders in new and complex ways.

Studies show that employees often use AI in unsanctioned ways, frequently utilizing publicly available LLMs and applications. Given the rapid pace of change, many organizations are still in the process of developing internal AI policies, security protocols, and usability cases. Leaders need to address how to manage the transition from personal to professional AI use and drive the necessary behavioral changes.

Leaders must uphold strong ethical standards in the deployment and use of AI.

8. *We need more human(e) leadership to navigate us through this time.*

The role of leadership in effectively navigating through this period cannot be overemphasized. While awareness of AI as a technology is essential, the required qualities to leverage the new opportunities are deeply human and even humane.

Critical leadership traits include:

- Trust: Build and maintain trust within the organization. Build AI systems and applications that increase rather than decrease trust.
- Empathy: Understand and address the concerns and emotions of employees as AI-based capabilities get rolled out and trigger subsequent changes.
- Purpose: Align AI initiatives with the organization's values and goals, connected to a clear sense of purpose.

- Ethical: Uphold strong ethical standards in the deployment and use of AI.
- Boundary-Spanning: Work across different departments and stakeholders to ensure cohesive AI strategies.

In summary, our research across our membership shows that they are optimistic but clear-eyed about AI. They feel a sense of urgency in developing the proper guardrails and effective governance in order to set employees free to experiment and innovate. They emphasize education and communication so leaders can make informed investment decisions aligning AI strategy with their organization's purpose. But even the skeptics are unwilling to risk sitting on the sidelines. This technology is evolving at an unprecedented pace, and those who fall too far behind are unlikely to experience a grace period to catch up. There is a clear preference to lead by building trust, expressing empathy, and aiming for positive change.

Abigail Kramer *is a community builder who has spent over three decades working with CIOs on strategy, organization, and technology evaluations at Kleiner Perkins' CIO Strategy Exchange, the Research Board, and elsewhere. Prior to co-founding Samudra (www.samudra.group), she orchestrated enterprise strategy and engagement with the cloud storage company, Box.*

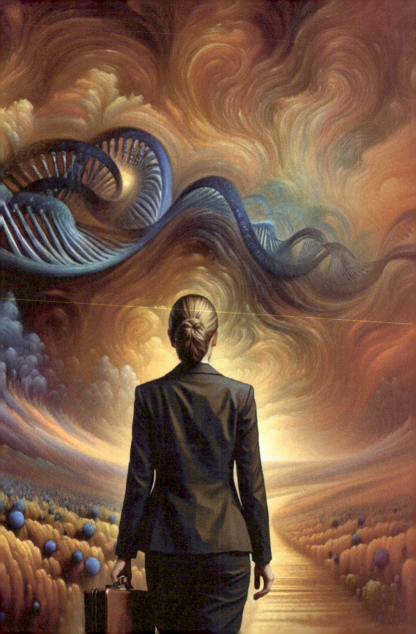

By Trudi West

Biographical Disruption

How Life's Challenges Shape Our Stories

"That was really awkward! Why would you make us do that?

That would never happen in real life!"

This was shouted at me during the first face-to-face workshop I had facilitated after Covid. I was working with a group of senior leaders that had previously only met virtually. In the run up to this workshop, they had asked for it to be more *experiential* and less *theoretical* – and that they wanted to be stretched. This is where I come in as that's what I do – I work with leaders to stretch their understanding of themselves through experiences, reflection and with just enough theory to hang their hat on

What had I 'made' him do that led to him to shout at me? I had invited him to check-in with a fellow participant for two minutes – in silence.

Much to his discomfort – this was real life. And an example of what I call an 'itchy armpit moment'. This is because high stress 'risky' environments can trigger the release of hormones like adrenaline, which activates the apocrine sweat glands especially prominent in the armpits. But mostly because, many years ago, my friend drove too fast around a roundabout. As she described her experience, her aunt asked, "*did you get itchy armpits?*". On reflection, she realised she had!

Where this comes from

I have been interested in what happens under pressure since my first career, as a runner and then as a broker on an open outcry trading floor. Now, as a development practitioner working with leaders, I am fascinated by how being under pressure impacts how we trust ourselves, make decisions, take risks, what we say and importantly, what we do. How we judge and justify under pressure reflects our integrity and our hypocrisies (West TEDx – link embedded).

To explore this more, I have developed *breaching experiments* which put on some pressure to see how I think, feel and act. I then use different methods to reflect

I am fascinated by how being under pressure impacts how we trust ourselves, make decisions, take risks, what we say and importantly, what we do.

on these experiences to understand better what goes on in those moments, and to discern what is really at risk – in here and out there. I have also been embedding *breaching experiments* within the leadership programmes I facilitate as experiential exercises which develop the capacity to notice habits, presumptions, and narratives.

Breaching Experiments

I believe that itchy armpit moments have the potential to *breach* our expectations, and even our identity. However, simply telling people to 'get out of your comfort zones more' is easy to say but putting it into practice can be difficult. Especially at work, when doing something different can *feel* risky 'in here' and may even be risky 'out there'. This is where *breaching experiments* provide a relatively safe way to breach our 'everyday' experience on purpose.

Garfinkel (1967) initially developed **breaching experiments** to "*cause trouble*" in order to reveal these

While breaching experiments can feel subjectively risky 'in here' – they are not objectively risky 'out there'.

background assumptions, expectancies and common knowledge that people took for granted and which underpinned everyday social life. This is because, in Garfinkel's view, *"we are all busy constructing a world in which we feel at home"* (p.113).

How do breaching experiments translate into every day, especially when they can feel so risky? By experimenting in relatively controlled ways outside of your every day, you are much more likely to be able to experiment inside it. While breaching experiments can *feel* subjectively risky *'in here'* – they are not objectively risky *'out there'*. Knowing this consciously means being able to pay attention to inner-narrations which inform *how* and *why* this might *feel* risky, and any presumptions being made about our own or others' expectations or behaviours. What beliefs are held, and which values are valued.

Breaching experiments help to interrupt our comfort zones and unsettle our mental short-cuts. This allows us to tune into our inner-narrations, and learn to distinguish between our hunches, the stories we tell ourselves and

perhaps even, the voice of our inner critic. Through these experiences, reflection and with just enough theory to hang our hats on, we can step back and see ourselves in action. We can then reflect on who we are, what we want and importantly what we do not want. Further reflection makes it possible to challenge presumptions about what we can and cannot do.

On one hand, breaching experiments provide a well-spring of narratives about judgement, power, criticism and perception of risk. On the other, they can develop hunches, curiosity and importantly, a greater sense of self. They also help uncover how these narrations may be limiting or indeed, liberating.

Change happens at the edges

The 'silence' exercise often brings up all sorts of responses. Some begin to gesture wildly, while others stare at the floor. Some write things down while others bond through choosing to make eye contact. In experiencing, and then reflecting on what they notice, participants are often surprised by the range of assumptions and inferences they can make in those two minutes. It quickly becomes apparent to everyone just how much their inner-narrations shape their experience beyond what is, in effect, a room full of people sitting together in silence for just two-minutes.

This is not about the ability to **read the room**. That is not the point of the exercise. That is the easy bit, as their experience is often tangible. As my colleague once whispered to me upon witnessing the two-minute exercise – "*they absolutely hate you right now*". It would be easy to conclude that as the exercise feels difficult, I should not *make* anyone do it. And if I wanted them to like me, I *would not* make them.

Finding the edge of the breach is part of the experiment. For example, another breaching experiment is to have dinner by yourself. When I did this, I quickly realised that having a phone or a book with me made it much easier. So, if you are going to try this – take them away. As it was, I ended up 'journalling' on the back of a napkin. I

The 'silence' exercise often brings up all sorts of responses. Some begin to gesture wildly, while others stare at the floor.

told myself a pedantic truth that was ok as it was neither a book nor a phone. Anything rather than face what was really going on – I didn't want people to feel sorry for me.

Recently, I suggested this breaching experiment during a workshop. One of the participants said that it would not be much of a stretch for him as he regularly travels to Kazakhstan for work. He often eats in restaurants without a book or a phone because he really enjoys having interesting conversations with the locals. I said that sounded quite adventurous, almost daring. He agreed heartily. I then asked where he lived – he said Coventry. I suggested he have dinner by himself on a Tuesday night, without a book or a phone in Coventry …. "oh no, bugger that! I'm not doing that!". His tale of Kazakhstan tells the story of a person who is adventurous and daring 'out there'. However, his reaction to having dinner alone in Coventry on a Tuesday evening said more about what feels risky for him 'in here'.

As well as the *2-min silence* and *dinner by yourself* experiment – you could try wearing an unexpected item of clothing all day without explanation, go to the cinema alone and watch whatever film is next, or drive

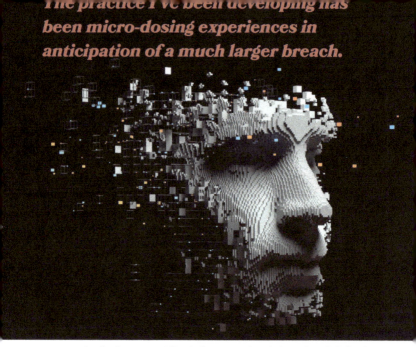

The practice I've been developing has been micro-dosing experiences in anticipation of a much larger breach.

at *precisely* the speed limit (presuming it is safe to). I find it is best just to get on with it and not think too deeply or too much about what you *think* will happen. Just decide to experiment and explore what occurs.

By doing something different *outside of your everyday* experience in relatively controlled ways, you are much more likely to be able to experiment *inside it*. You will learn to differentiate what feels risky 'in here' from what is (or isn't) inherently risky 'out there' because you can hear, challenge and develop the stories you are telling yourself. The insights that arise can be so rich and rewarding that eventually, experiments and reflection becomes *part of your everyday*.

Biographical Disruption

I now realise that the practice I have been developing has, in effect, been micro-dosing experiences in anticipation of a much larger breach. Beyond insights, narrations, and hunches – there are some experiences which not only breach – they **biographically disrupt**.

While micro-dosing is usually associated with the practice of consuming very low, sub-hallucinogenic doses of a psychedelic substance, this metaphor works for both my wider doctoral inquiry into trust in self, but also *specifically*, as part of a *biographically disrupting* diagnosis caught early, but nevertheless, aggressive form of breast cancer.

Bury (1982) describes the diagnosis of a chronic illness as "*disruptions in biography which are, at one and the same time, disruptions of social relationships and the ability to mobilise material resources*" (p180). A diagnosis of this kind can evoke a search for meaning from past events to try and answer, "*why me? why now?*" while expectations and plans for the future are re-examined. Pranka (2018) describes how a life-threatening illness breaks an individual's social and cultural experience by

I started treatment feeling well but it was necessary for me to be very poorly to become invisibly better.

threatening his or her self-identity. When reflecting in my journal, what emerged was that it was not the diagnosis itself, but rather, the biopsy was enough to create biographical disruption:

"Then that puncture of the biopsy. That's when everything changed. Adrenaline ran through my body, and I cried. I don't think it was fear for the future or life ending stuff. I felt a sense of shame that I hadn't really appreciated what others before me had gone through. When my Dad had lung cancer – I focused more on the details of the cancer, not realising the biographical disruption he could have experienced. This is the stuff of biographical disruption. It's not just a lump – it's an infinite number of potentials, of moments that we will now experience. People to meet and stories to hear. And I notice I don't actually want to talk – I don't have the language and I'm not ready to find one. I left the hospital with their words: cancer, operation, radiotherapy, and chemo, along with suspicious and "you strike me as a

fighter". They're all quite heavy words and that's more than enough to be getting on with. Even if it's just a storm in a teacup – there is a storm and there's still a teacup"
West Journal 28thJuly 2023 – Biopsy Day

I have been asked if biographical disruption is not just another name for trauma, or if my inquiry is about learning how to heal from such an event. For me, it isn't. For example, so much has come from the impact of chemotherapy. I started treatment feeling well but it was necessary for me to be very poorly to become invisibly better. In that time, I have reflected on who I am, how I see myself, how much I can tolerate and importantly, the precious finite value of time and energy. While there have been traumatic moments, and without doubt healing is required – this work is not about trauma or healing. It is much closer to learning and self-determination.

Biographical disruption is not a one-off event – it creates a series of breaching experiences. The past, present and future being challenged every day, requiring reflection on what has been taken for granted, or moral positions unearthed – to explore how things are different and what *could* be different (Denzin, 2018, 197). And then what is needed to actually think, feel or *do* something different (Fletcher & Pine, 2012).

With reflection, nascent patterns begin to coalesce and connect what otherwise would remain disconnected.

Intuitively – biographical disruption stretches beyond the bounds of chronic illness. Many of you reading this will recognise your own biographical disruptions, for example, through illness, an accident, or the loss of a loved one in whatever way they feel lost to you. You may have gone through a divorce, or redundancy. And many of you might not.

Micro-dosing breaching experiences

By using different methods to reflect on *breaching experiences*, it is possible to notice where thoughts run in the moment. With reflection, nascent patterns begin to coalesce and connect what otherwise would remain disconnected. Invariably, this provides *enough* momentum to think, feel or do something different on the ground.

One method I use draws on Turner-Vesselago's (1995) technique for writers – 'Freefall Writing' (in Marshall, 2008). **Writing to understand** helps to reflect on experience and gives rise to new insights. This emergent process regularly generates truly new 'aha' moments

(Gopnick, 2000) and symbolic growth experiences (Frick, 1983). These can occur as I am writing or after some time, upon further reflection. Marshall describes the process of Freefall as "*keep the hand moving; don't cross out; don't worry about spelling, punctuation, grammar; don't think – write; show, don't tell – give the sensuous detail; and go where the energy is, which may be fear-ward*" (p.11). Below are the specific instructions I give to participants during a program:

> ## Try some freefall writing....
>
> - Given it is **essential** you **reflect** on your **experience** for **deeper learning** that **lasts longer**...
> - Put pen to paper and write
> - And then keep writing.
> - If you run out of things to write – write 'I'm running out of things to write....' until you think of something else to write
>
> *"when I reflect on this experience, what I notice is..."*

People often ask if they could type instead of write. I'd say – try writing first. There is something about writing which connects the words as they flow from the pen. Plus, we tend to associate typed words with written communication with others. Subconsciously, you may become aware of spellchecks and formatting. No-one will read this except you, and maybe not even then. It is intended

Speaking-to-understand helps identify and express inner-narrations and presumptions out loud.

to bring the thoughts out and potentially, bring them together. It is not to *present* them.

Once, I was working with a network of CEOs. After introducing freefall writing as a method of reflection, one of them asked afterwards "*how can I trust what I've just written?*" He explained that he had struggled with imposter syndrome for most of his career, and he had not always trusted himself. I asked him how he *felt* as he was writing – "*I trusted myself to write what I needed, whatever that needed to be*". He seemed genuinely surprised at himself.

Speaking to understand helps reflect and make connections as the words arrive in my mouth, creating clarity through emergent articulation. In conversation with those I trust, *speaking to understand* helps identify and express inner-narrations and presumptions out loud, and often provides potential for sharing and connecting hunches, anecdotes and moral challenges. We can hear our words judging and justifying, ourselves and others. Spack (1985) might describe this as *serious gossip* (as opposed to *malicious gossip*) and creates "*a catalyst of*

social process. [...] It provides opportunity for self-disclosure and for examination of moral decisions" (p. 34). Serious gossip is not just passing the time with small talk as that would undermine its value in being able to share experiences as part of a social system. It helps us make sense of our underdeveloped *latent dissent*, especially in confusing social systems. Speaking with trusted others develops the *articulation of dissent* (Kassing, 1997).

These *emerging* conversations are key on programs as it is where much of the learning happens – where participants create their own *content* and make connections for themselves and with each other. Continuing in action learning sets provides ongoing opportunity to develop this method. There is also the old-fashioned *kitchen table confidante* – someone to talk to that has your interest at heart (thank you Lynn).

It is important to note that these methods will not necessarily provide definitive answers – there are no certainties, and nothing is absolutely 'true'. Yet they do provide *enough* to help locate a *hunch* – and with *enough* inferencing potency to provide a catalyst for further reflection or action.

A Working Theory

My working theory is that there is potential to breach, transform or threaten our self-identity *at any time*. And using the micro-dosing metaphor – *breaching experiences* correspond with Bury's *biographical disruption* of a chronic illness. They are simply on a different scale.

I also notice they differ in how they are authenticated to others. There is often less to substantiate and more to discount when describing learning that occurs during a breaching experience, especially when compared to a medical diagnosis, for example. Who is going to argue with me when I say having breast cancer has changed the way I think, feel or act? And yet I have been challenged when explaining *how* change has happened as a result of having dinner by oneself, or the aha moment that occurred when wearing a hat for no reason.

In combining these, I would even venture to extend Bury's concept of *biographical disruption* to *autoethnographical disruption*. This encompasses reflections beyond the *biography* (the life story of a person written by someone else), or *autobiography* as *a confessional tale* (Sparkes, 2020, p6). Autoethnographies show people in the process of figuring out what to do, how to live, and what their struggles mean (Bochner & Ellis, 2006, p. 111, in Ellis, 2007, p26). By extending biographical disruption with the additional emphasis on the 'ethno' aspect it is possible to draw explicitly on personal breaching experiences which intentionally '*illustrate and interrogate cultural beliefs, practices and identities*' (Adams & Hermann, 2020, p2).

My *intention* is to show *how* significant breaches can occur when eating dinner by yourself, having a conversation with a stranger, or with the puncture of a biopsy needle – just some of the many disruptions experienced that can fundamentally shift thinking, feeling and action.

A fully referenced version of this article is available from editor@dl-q.com

Trudi West *has a keen interest in what drives thinking, feeling and action, particularly for leaders being pulled in many directions, with few 'right' answers. She creates trusting yet challenging learning environments for leaders to experience, make sense and do something different for themselves and others.*

By Zoryna O'Donnell and
Theresa Dzendrowskyj

Reflective Practice for Leaders and Their Teams

Definition: What is reflective practice?

Reflective practice is principally a process of self-analysis where individuals and groups reflect on their thoughts, feelings and actions in order to understand, evaluate and interpret events and experiences in which they are involved. This process is an intentional, deliberate and in-depth consideration of the events, situations, thoughts, words and actions chosen because they can be used to modify future practice in order to achieve even better outcomes. This intentional reflection on experience is essential for effective learning, continuous improvement and future planning.

"Reflection gives the brain an opportunity to pause amidst the chaos, untangle, and sort through observations and experiences."

It is important to remember that reflective practice is an active and dynamic process, a series of stages that continually recycle.

Building on the Gibbs' Reflective Cycle (1998), Julie Hay (2007), suggested the following six stages of the reflection process:

1. Capturing events as they occur.
2. Reviewing specific events.
3. Reviewing a series of events to look for patterns.
4. Planning ahead to incorporate learning points generally.
5. Planning ahead for specific events.
6. Implementing resulting learning.

In the workplace, leaders and their teams can consider the following practices:

- reflecting '*on*' action (past experiences and situations);
- reflecting '*in*' action (on an event or a situation as it happens); and
- reflecting '*for*' action (on future events or situations and on actions that they may wish to take in the future).

Why now?

In today's VUCA[1] world, where our attention span is reportedly shrinking, reflection should be seen as a key competency of effective leadership.

> *"Reflection gives the brain an opportunity to pause amidst the chaos, untangle, and sort through observations and experiences."*
>
> **Dr. R. Cooper, neuroscientist and leadership advisor**

What are the benefits of reflective practice for leaders and their teams?

There are four essential skills that underpin successful reflective practice in the workplace:

- ***self-awareness*** – the ability to focus on ourselves, our strengths and limitations, and how our thoughts, emotions judgements and actions do or do not align with our internal and external standards (for example, our values, organizational culture, societal norms or law).

- ***careful observation*** – paying attention to, and noticing, key aspects (including the meaning) of our experience and the situation as a whole. Then thinking more deeply about what we observed (for example, by asking ourselves: What worked and what did not?

---

1 Volatile, uncertain, complex and ambiguous.

Reflective practice was embedded into individual performance reviews and team meetings. As a result, team communication, morale, collaboration and performance are steadily improving.

Why did I and others behave the way we did?).

- ***critical thinking*** – making judgements based on reasoning, considering options and evaluating them using specific criteria, questioning assumptions, both our own and that of others, and drawing well-founded conclusions.
- ***flexible response*** – being able to adapt our style, approach and behaviour in response to complex, uncertain or unpredictable circumstances or changes as they come.

Our coaching clients who use reflective practice told us about the following benefits for their teams and the whole organizations:

- Client A from a public sector organization was asked to turn around an underperforming team with a track record of long-lasting inter-personal conflicts.

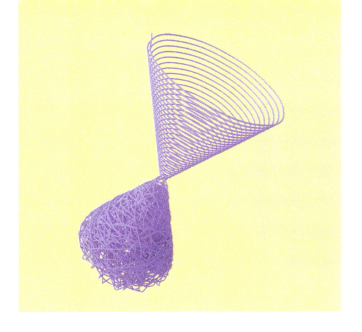

She used reflective practice conversations with the relevant individuals to create a greater level of their self-awareness about the nature and impact of specific behaviours and attitudes on work performance. This was followed by whole team discussions which widened the perspective on problems experienced by the team and helped to develop strategies to deal with conflicts and to improve collaboration within the team itself and with other teams and departments. Reflective practice was embedded into individual performance reviews and team meetings. As a result, team communication, morale, collaboration and performance are steadily improving.

- A number of strategic decisions resulted in a review and re-design of the portfolio of products and services in a technology company of Client L. This presented a challenge of facilitating fast learning and strengthening the capabilities of the teams affected by changes, while continuing to provide high quality customer care. Reflective practice was used in these teams as a tool to help them identify their strengths and limitations in relation to this challenge and to find the most efficient ways of learning and upskilling both on an individual and team levels. One of such ways was designating separate team members to focus on gaining different knowledge and skills and then sharing their learning with the rest of the team. According to Client L, this helped to embed the required knowledge and skills fast and deeply, while also developing the communication and collaboration skills of all team members.

- Reflective practice provides opportunities for professional growth and development. As Client N put it, "the coaching space allowed time for deep reflection and time to put together a set of articulated ideas, which I have applied to my personal development

agenda with much success. I am now operating with greater confidence and stronger collaboration, leading to more doors of opportunity that traditionally have not been available to me prior to this experience."

- Having experienced reflective practice during his coaching sessions, Client R is now using it to stimulate his own leadership development. He also introduced it to other members of the senior leadership team of his organization which is operating in the education sector. Since the beginning of the current academic year, Client R and his colleagues implemented a number of improvements to their workplace and leadership practice which were identified through reflective practice.

By using reflective practice, leaders and their teams can further enhance their skills as well as develop their

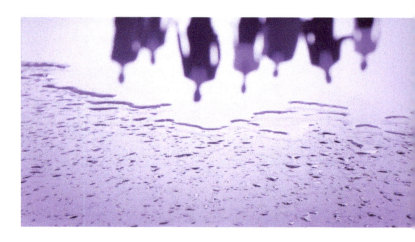

higher mental functions such as problem-solving and decision-making which will help them reach their goals more efficiently.

Team reflective practice also helps to capitalize on benefits of collective intelligence – the body of knowledge that grows out of a group of people working together which cannot exist on an individual level. Client P, who is leading an innovation and disruption department of a global engineering company, is using reflective practice as part of regular "insight and inspiration" discussions with his own teams and cross-functional project teams. Many innovative solutions and breakthroughs were born during these discussions.

There is a growing body of evidence highlighting the use and benefits of reflection in a variety of settings. These include health and social care, education, customer care and leadership development.

Team reflective practice also helps to capitalize on benefits of collective intelligence – the body of knowledge that grows out of a group of people working together which cannot exist on an individual level.

For example, Giada Di Stephano and colleagues[2] analysed evidence gathered in ten experimental studies with a total sample size of 4,340 people, conducted across different environments, geographies, and populations. They concluded that reflecting on accumulated experience generates higher performance outcomes than accumulating additional experience alone and pointed out that reflecting on what has been learned can increase performance by as much as 23%. The results of this study also suggest that the way in which people engage in reflection may play a major role in its effectiveness as a learning tool. It was established that articulating their reflections by participants of the study helped them to deepen information processing and achieve a stronger positive impact on their performance.

---

2   published by Di Stephano et al,(2014 and 2016). (https://ideasforleaders.com/Ideas/how-reflection-aids-performance-the-thinker-as-learner/)

What are the barriers to reflective practice in the workplace?

There is plenty of evidence to suggest that reflective practice is an effective learning tool helping to achieve performance improvement in individuals and teams. However, according to authors of the article "Why Leaders Don't Learn from Success" (Gino, F. and Pisano, P.) HBR, (2011), organizations that use it are the exception rather than the norm.

Why?

The six most common reasons for not using reflective practice which we hear from our clients include the following:

- *(Perceived) lack of time* – "most of the time I am way too busy to find even a few minutes to catch my breath, never mind reflections".
- *Lack of skill and know-how* – "I have heard about the benefits of reflective practice and even read about a few models, but could not decide which one to use. And the process itself sounded too complicated for my liking."
- *Organizational culture* – "we are not allowed to indulge in "navel-gazing" in my company."
- *Environment* – "I am working in the open plan office – not the best place for reflections!"

- **Motivation** – "I "gave a go" to reflections after one of the training courses I attended, but it felt a bit weird and I could not see any positive changes. I gave up after two weeks."
- **Ourselves** "I am not a reflection man, I am an action man!"

The same six barriers to reflection were also highlighted in the Reflective Practice Toolkit published by the Cambridge University Libraries.

We have to acknowledge that, while our appreciation of reflective practice as a means for meeting the challenges of today's digital world is growing, our ability to reflect is not necessarily an inherent attribute of every individual – whether or not he or she is in a position of leadership. Cynthia Roberts, (Purdue University), points out, that this ability "must be cultivated over time, and unless one is actively engaged in the practice of reflection, it is doubtful that this capability will develop on its own."

So, we added a **seventh barrier** to the list: often reflective practice is not used consistently and long enough to realize its full benefits and to become a habit – a regularly repeated behaviour that requires little or no thought and is learned rather than innate. This may explain why some people say that they have tried reflective practice but it did not work for them, so they did not bother any more.

Cultivation and habit formation are therefore critical to using reflective practice as a sustainable and valuable tool.

What are the models of reflective practice?

Most models of reflective practice are based on the famous psychological and educational theory known as **Kolb's Learning Cycle** which offers a simple explanation of the concept of reflective learning.

As illustrated by Figure 1, a learning event starts with "An experience", followed by "Reviewing/Reflecting on the experience", followed by "Concluding/Learning from the experience", then "Implementing/Trying out what you have learned". This is an ongoing cycle which can be repeated many times.

In his systematic review and revision of Kolb's model, Dr. Thomas Morris (Bath Spa University) argued that, while Kolb's model remains the principal and most influential model in experiential learning theory, it has a number of shortcomings including lack of empirical evidence which Morris looked to address in a subsequent study.

Based on the results of this review, a revision to Kolb's 1984 model by Morris is illustrated by Figure 2.

Whilst this revised model is based on studies of experiential learning, they are in contexts that represented

Figure 1. Kolb's Learning Cycle (1984)

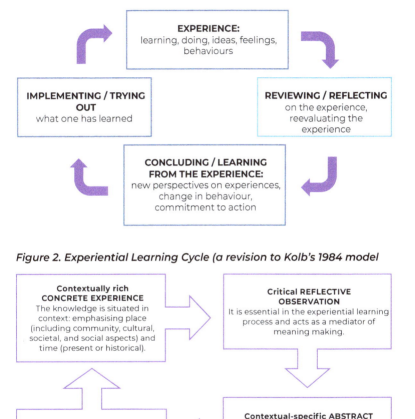

Figure 2. Experiential Learning Cycle (a revision to Kolb's 1984 model

out-of-classroom experiences and therefore, more empirical studies are needed to test its assumptions, particularly in the workplace.

Gibbs's Reflective Cycle, Learning by Doing (1998) is more comprehensive than Kolb's model and provides prompting questions throughout the process.

This model illustrated by Figure 3 is a good way to work through both a stand-alone experience and situations people go through regularly, for example meetings with a team they have to collaborate with.

Figure 3. Gibbs's Reflective Cycle (1998)

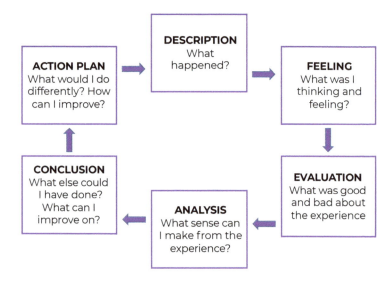

Organizations that use reflective practice are the exception rather than the norm.

This format guides a methodical and thorough evaluation of an experience, making it simpler to pinpoint key elements. It promotes self-awareness and holistic learning and drives people to develop action plans and future strategies. It is also flexible enough to be used in various contexts – for example, in business, healthcare, social care and education.

However, while this model is systematic and relatively simple to follow, it may take a lot of time to go through all six steps, so most people who are time-short may avoid regular reflective practice as they simply don't have the time to make it a habit.

Boud Reflection Model illustrated by Figure 4 (overleaf) was developed by David Boud, Rosemary Keogh and David Walker in 1985. It is one of the simplest (and quickest to use) models of reflection. It focuses on learning by reflecting on one's practice to better understand their activities and their background in order to improve what they do with their work responsibilities.

This model of reflective practice can help develop different kinds of perspectives which take account of human emotions helping people separate the useful feelings

Figure 4. Boud Reflection Model (1985)

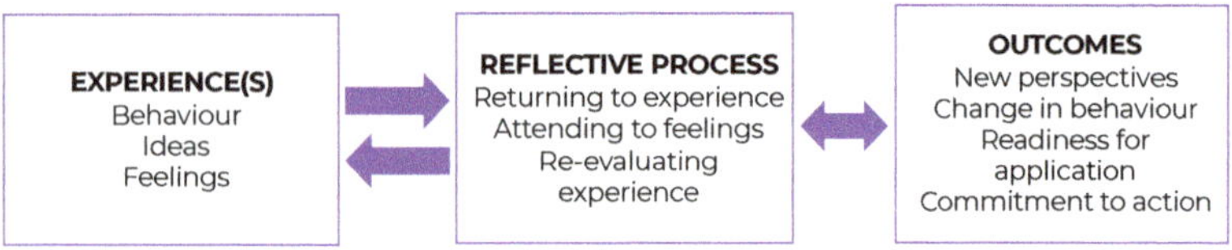

that are part of their work actions and decision-making, so that they are able to control emotions and use them to their advantage in the performance of professional activities.

However, this model does not elaborate on what reflection might consist of, or how the learning might translate back into experience of workplace practice.

The "What" Model of reflective practice illustrated by Figure 5 was created by Professors Rolfe, Freshwater and Jasper (2001), and was originally conceptualized around nursing practice. However, it proved to be useful in other contexts too, for example in education, social care and also business. It describes an iterative process consisting of three simple questions which require comprehensive reflective answers.

Some of the potential difficulties in using this model are that it requires a lot of self-awareness, situation awareness, "reflection on reflection" as well as time in

Figure 5. The "What" Model of Rolfe et al. (2001)

WHAT? Descriptive	**SO WHAT?** Knowledge & meaning	**NOW WHAT?** Plan of action
... happened? ... are the key aspects of this experience? ... was my role in this situation? ... was I trying to achieve? ... were my reactions to it – then and now? ... were the responses of others – then and now? ... was good / bad about the experience? ... is my purpose for revisiting this experience?	... does this mean? ... informed my actions/behaviour? ... other knowledge and experience can I bring to the situation? ...could I do differently? ... is my new understanding of the situation now? ... other broader issues have arisen?	... are the implications for future experiences? ... are the broader issues I need to reflect on/consider? ... do I need to do to improve the situation / prevent recurrence? ... are the broader issues that need to be considered if action is to be successful? ... is my action plan going forwards? ... can I do to transfer this learning to other contexts?

order to ask all "the right questions" or questions that help reflection. To some extent, this limitation can be mitigated by using The "What" Model in dialogue with another person (a colleague, a manager, or another professional, for example a coach or a mentor) where both can challenge each other to reflect deeper, triggering a dialectic approach.

It was due to the different challenges we encountered with each of the models described above, that we developed, with Lindsey Popplewell, our **EASY Model**

> ## *"Our brain is like Velcro for negative experiences, but Teflon for positive ones"*

of reflective practice in 2023. Like other models of reflective practice, the EASY Model is rooted in the Kolb's Learning Cycle. And yet, this model is different by design from other models because it is also informed by insights from applied neuroscience, behaviour science and positive psychology. It is also quick and easy to follow.

As illustrated by Figure 6, this model utilises a combination of an acronym and kinaesthetic physical mnemonic (memory device) which uses fingers to remember the acronym EASY where each letter stands for one of the four steps:

- **E** – **E**stablish your intention – what do you want to achieve / what area of your leadership you wish to focus on?
- **A** – **A**cknowledge what went well – and continue doing that.
- **S** – **S**tep up your game – reflect on what you have learned and consider what you can do differently, perhaps even better, to enhance your leadership impact.
- **Y** – **Y**our commitment to act – decide what you will do and do it!

Figure 6. The EASY Model of Reflective Practice (2023)

• **E**stablishing your intention

• **A**cknowledging what went well

• **S**tepping up your game

• **Y**our commitment to act

Thumbs up – done!

The EASY Model of reflective practice is effective because:

• Establishing intention focuses our limited executive attention on what matters to us and helps in action planning and protecting the pursuit of our current goal from distractions and temptations. Setting intention also provides accountability and allows us to make proactive choices.

• Acknowledging what went well helps to confront and overcome our negativity bias.

> *"Our brain is like Velcro for negative experiences, but Teflon for positive ones"*
> **Rick Hanson, neuropsychologist and author**

We can overcome this bias by reminding ourselves about our achievements and successes. Acknowledging what went well serves to quieten our inner critic, calm our limbic system, and bring our parasympathetic nervous system online. It will also help to boost our self-compassion, self-esteem and confidence in preparation for the next step.

- Stepping-up our game brings our prefrontal cortex online which intelligently regulates our thoughts, actions and emotions through extensive connections with other brain regions, and helps us decide what we can do differently to achieve even better results. It helps us to prepare for future actions. During this step we are "slowing down in order to speed up" – we are using our "system 2 thinking" (slow, deliberate and conscious) to create our action plan and to move it into our "system 1 thinking" (habit-forming, fast, automatic and effortless) (Kahneman, 2012).

- Your commitment to act is not just about deciding what to do and when. Any commitment is only true when we act upon it. This step builds on a positive state and momentum of the previous steps thus helping us to move from decision to action.

The process could be repeated with a new intention to explore another aspect of the same situation or behaviour, or to reflect on a new one.

It is recommended to massage each finger while going through the corresponding step of the EASY model. According to research[3], finger massage is conducive to improving intelligence and sharpening the mind. And regular finger exercise can improve brain circulation and form new exciting points and connections in the brain, which is beneficial to the improvement of understanding, memory and thinking.

To conclude:

There are many more models of reflective practice. Michelle Lucas in her new book "Creating the Reflective Habit: A Practical Guide for Coaches, Mentors and Leaders" presents some of them and offers a practical toolkit which shows how to create a sustainable reflective habit in individuals and organizations.

Essentially, it does not really matter which model leaders and their teams use as long as it works for them and they build reflective practice into their daily/weekly routine and use it consistently for continuous improvement of themselves and their team.

Reflective practice does not have to take a lot of time. According to a 2021 study on habit formation and routine published by Jan Keller and colleagues, "piggy-backing" on existing routines helps to form a new habit more quickly and easily. This is useful to know

---

3   published by Bisio. A., et al (2017)

According to research, finger massage is conducive to improving intelligence and sharpening mind.

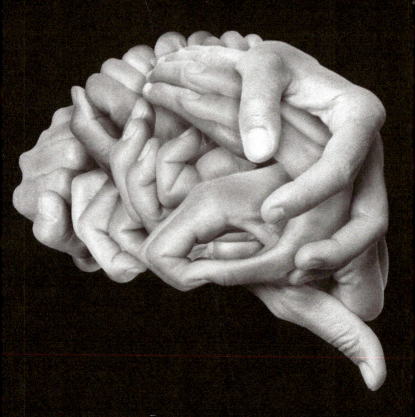

when considering the best ways to create a reflective practice habit. Try reflecting whilst brushing your teeth!

Alternatively, it is possible to integrate reflections into everyone's daily work, (for example, when moving from one activity to the next, pausing for a brief moment to reflect on what was accomplished and the impact it had), or to include reflection in team meetings and project reviews. The key skill is to make it part of your routine. Create and maintain the habit!

Working with a coach or a mentor is another way to help leaders and their teams build lasting reflection skills which could be used effectively in the workplace and beyond.

A table of Further Reading on this topic is available from editor@dl-q.com

Zoryna O'Donnell *is a leadership consultant and executive coach specialising in neuroscience-informed leadership and management development, change management and wellbeing programmes. She is a founder and director of L&M Plus Consulting (https:// www.lmplusconsulting.com) and a Fellow of the Institute of Leadership.*

Theresa Dzendrowskyj, *(Ph.D, MBA), specialises in applied neuroscience in business, health and wellbeing as an executive coach in leadership and strategic change. As a mindfulness meditation teacher, she also uses mind-training interventions to support focus, clarity, resilience and decision making.*

By Paul Williamson

Long Story Short

Leadership Development at ATG Entertainment

t was the hottest September day since 1911. The date was 13th September 2016, and inside a stiflingly warm studio theatre in Wimbledon, South London, something extraordinary was happening...

Having completed a two-year leadership development programme called *Rising Stars*, eight young ATG leaders were taking their moment in the spotlight, and speaking to an invited audience of senior managers, family, friends, and colleagues. Each Rising Star took to the stage that day to tell their personal leadership story

The business revolves around telling engaging stories and expressing thoughts, actions, and emotions 'in the moment' to connect human beings

Despite having had an identical brief, no two presentations were the same. Each young leader showed vulnerability, each shared moments of insight, learning, and challenge, and all of them spoke with passion, confidence, and purpose, in a voice totally their own.

It was the first time an event like this had taken place in the organization, and looking back, one of the reasons it packed such a punch, was because, at some fundamental level, it was so congruent with the purpose of the business.

ATG Entertainment owns or operates 64 iconic venues worldwide, produces shows and sells tickets through a large ticketing operation. At its heart though, whether it is through theatre, music, or comedy, the business revolves around telling engaging stories and expressing thoughts, actions, and emotions 'in the moment' to connect human beings in a darkened auditorium. The self-same thing was happening on that oppressively hot day in 2016, and the impact would prove to be swift and far-reaching.

It stirred something inside the audience that day, particularly senior managers within the business. They looked at these young, impressive leaders, and they felt inspired. They wanted to know how they too could engage an audience like that. They were intrigued by the concepts and learning experiences shared that day, and they wanted to experience something similar. A movement had started.

Interestingly, received wisdom would have us believe that cultural change within an organization must happen at the top first and work down. The reverse was true for us, and future development programmes were sanctioned on the strength of the success of *Rising Stars* – which proves you can positively influence leadership culture from any position in the system.

The *Rising Stars* story started in 2014, with a seemingly straightforward objective around developing our 'leaders of tomorrow'. We wanted to spot and retain talented people early in their careers and remove barriers preventing internal progression. We wanted to break down silos within the business too and create a trusted talent pipeline.

We also wanted to involve as much of the business as possible in the identification and selection of talent. Anyone could apply for the scheme, as long as their application was endorsed by their line manager and another senior sponsor within the business. This encouraged discussions to take place throughout ATG about performance, ambition, leadership potential and learning. Key senior managers were also involved in the selection process. In readiness for the programme launch in 2014, we trained a group of managers to be able to have one-to-one coaching conversations with our *Rising Stars*, and further support their growth. For this, we partnered with the Academy of Executive Coaching (AoEC), who ran an in-house certificate programme for us. This element has gone from strength-to-strength, and in 2021, sixteen managers completed the AoEC Practitioner Diploma in Executive Coaching, becoming qualified executive coaches. An ATG internal coaching faculty is now in operation supporting all our Rising Stars, and providing coaching services to the wider business.

Care is taken selecting each cohort of Rising Stars. First, there is an application form which asks key questions, testing leadership potential and alignment with the company's vision and values. Stage two is a presentation and interview to a small panel. Here we set applicants a creative presentation brief, often asking them to play with metaphor to help describe their aspirations.

As the years progressed, leaders who had completed Rising Stars joined an alumni group and got actively involved in the selection process for future participants. Alumni now score application forms, sit on *Rising Stars* interview panels, and some joined our coaching faculty, all of which creates a virtuous circle of development and support.

Each cohort is carefully chosen, ensuring there is a good mix of people from different disciplines across the organization. We also aim to get a good geographical spread, with people taking part everywhere from Torquay to Glasgow. This is important for a big organization like ours. Building a groupwide network helps to break down silos, give people a clearer sense of the bigger picture, and a greater feeling of belonging.

Alumni now sit on Rising Stars interview panels, and some joined our coaching faculty, all of which creates a virtuous circle of development and support.

We have found that an early focus on presentation skills seems to accelerate leadership growth with our emerging leaders. Early on, we ask our Rising Stars to prepare a five-minute presentation on something they are passionate about – and we have had everything from Lego to Lord of the Rings! This is often an early turning point for many participants. So much of what naturally comes out of a person when they are talking about something they are passionate about, once identified and remembered, can be applied to any presentation. We share grounding techniques to lower the stakes for people, so they are able to be at ease and present in a way that feels true to who they are.

Before the group do their 'passion' presentations we always do an exercise where they close their eyes, and are then taken on a guided experience, which culminates in them identifying a time, or place, where they have felt calm, safe, confident, and loved. They are asked to conjure up an image and feel it somatically – something that can be summoned up, when required. I will never forget one of our Rising Stars lost his way during his presentation – but rather than panic and potentially give up, he took a moment, paused, closed his eyes, remembered his grounding image from the morning exercise (for him – it was his young kids)... He was able to quickly re-group and get back into the flow of his presentation.

I co-facilitated the programme with an external coach/facilitator called Nicky Stone. Nicky brings knowledge, stories and expertise from other sectors and industries, and I bring over 25 years of experience of working at ATG. In another example of the virtuous circle, I now have an L&D Manager called Rosie Preston, who was herself a Rising Star in Cohort 3 of the programme. Rosie now fulfils the internal facilitation role, as I turn my attention to new programmes and initiatives.

A series of day-long workshops on a variety of subjects from creative thinking to time management are delivered (around six a year) as part of *Rising Stars*. Crucially though, at the beginning of every session, participants are given time to check in with one another, talk about how they have applied the learning from previous sessions and share the highs and lows. This, without a doubt, has helped to create a psychologically safe environment and enabled our leaders to show vulnerability, gain support and grow as individuals and as a collective.

At the beginning of the second year, Rising Stars complete a Hogan Personality Assessment and are given feedback on the results in a one-to-one coaching session. Being aware of your 'derailers' and knowing how certain strengths can be overplayed, causing reputational damage, is powerful learning. Raising awareness of this and finding ways to effectively 'turn down the volume' on derailing behaviour can be a real game-changer. Having a report that essentially tells you what your drivers are and what needs to be present in your life and work to create a sense of fulfilment, can also be reassuring and instructive, unlocking insight into why a person might get drawn to certain types of work, or equally, the kind of work someone might struggle with.

Following the success of *Rising Stars* I was asked to develop a leadership development programme for senior managers at ATG. This eventually became Leading Lights, which consists of a Hogan's personality assessment with feedback prior to commencement, two separate residential weeks of learning and six one-to-one coaching sessions with an external executive coach in between.

Leading Lights has been described as 'transformational' and 'life-changing' by participants. The first week focuses on emotional intelligence and coaching skills for leaders and week two is themed around storytelling and creativity in leadership. In addition to our core facilitation team of Zoe Cogan, Caroline Lansbury and

Leading Lights has been described as 'transformational' and 'life changing' by participants.

Nicky Stone, each week includes sessions with influential master coaches, thought leaders and authors like Dr John Blakey, Sheila Campbell-Lloyd, Dr Sarah Hill and Dr Carole Pemberton. These incredible contributors not only share their insights on key subjects such as trust, neuroscience, childhood story and resilience, they also model how to hold a space, how to listen, ask questions and be curious.

The slightest trace of self-doubt, indecision, or a lack of commitment and the horse will stop and refuse to move until you are bringing your best.

Some people doubt the long-term impact a leadership programme can have on a person, and maybe the effect can be short-lived for some, but for others it can be something else entirely. I remember one *Leading Lights* participant describing himself as 'authoritarian' and 'a bit of a dictator' prior to attending the course. He also reported severe pain in his neck and shoulder – a physical manifestation of the stress he felt at work. Learning coaching skills and hearing from successful people who used coaching as a way of leading, led to a transformational change in him. He realized how wasteful it was resorting to 'telling people what to do' and not tapping into the creativity and resourcefulness of his team. He also realized the negative impact his behaviour was having on people that worked for him, and wanted to change. He bravely went back to his venue and told people what he had learned, the changes he wanted to make, and sought their help. He asked them to tell him if his 'old' behaviours started to creep back in. Sure enough, they told him when they saw signs of retrenchment, and he would thank them, go off to his office, shut

the door, and ground himself, using mindfulness techniques he had learned on the programme. A year later he said, 'If you talked to people that worked for me pre – and post-*Leading Lights*, they'll tell you I'm a different person.' Seven years later and he is still maintaining a more people-focused approach, and reports that he has not experienced the pain in his neck and shoulder since doing *Leading Lights*.

By 2018 we had two highly successful leadership development programmes, but many middle managers felt excluded. In response, we launched *Interval* in November 2019.

'Interval' means 'the space between two things', and the concept behind the programme was to provide a space for experienced managers to take time out, reflect, and engage with up-to-date leadership approaches and techniques, connect with their purpose and lead with greater authenticity and confidence. I co-facilitate the programme with Sarah Rozenthuler, a chartered psychologist, leadership coach and author of 'Powered by Purpose'. Here we use David Kantor's Structural Dynamics and participants complete a bMaps psychometric to examine behavioural patterns in low and high stakes. Knowledge of Kantor's model provides leaders a chance to read rooms and expand their behavioural and communicative repertoire to get better outcomes.

The really unique feature of *Interval* is an outdoor workshop in Staffordshire with Jude Jennison and her herd of horses. The horse workshops are incredibly powerful and provide experiences that stay in the memory a lifetime (just like great theatre). What is so fascinating is that the degree to which a horse will allow you to lead them, depends on a number of key things. The first is the energy you bring and whether the horses feel safe with you. Then it is the quality of the relationship you build – do you take time to build rapport, show respect and build trust? Or do you move straight into action and attempt to 'pull' the horse along? You also need to be clear on direction, make decisions and confidently bring the horse with you. The slightest trace of self-doubt, inde-

cision, or a lack of commitment and the horse will stop
and refuse to move until you are bringing your best. Jude
is incredibly skilled as a coach and facilitator and can
quickly draw out the parallels between what is happening
in the arena with her horses and what might be taking
place for you in the workplace. With uncanny accuracy
the horses provide crystal-clear non-verbal feedback to
participants, which, once interpreted, can be applied to
human interactions back in the office. The results have
been profound. One participant told us,

> 'I was very sceptical prior to the horse work-
> shop but was absolutely blown away by what I
> gained from that session. I like to think it has
> made me both a better leader, but also a better
> manager who continually supports and encour-
> ages their team to be better leaders and team
> members themselves.'

In addition to these four core programmes, we have also
added *Open Space*, a virtual programme, which concen-
trates on inclusive leadership. Led by coach, facilitator
and author Salma Shah, *Open Space* has been designed
to help leaders build equitable, inclusive, and diverse
workplaces for all. This programme creates a safe space
for a culturally diverse group of leaders to share different lived experience, explore identity, belonging and

Leaders need to work on themselves just as hard as they work on projects, tasks and other people.

how this can impact on our personal and work systems. It ends with a showcase event, where participants will invite allies and influential ATG leaders to join them, hear what they have learned, how they have applied it, and what more can be done to support this tremendously important work.

So, what has been learned from the story so far here at ATG Entertainment?

1. **Leadership development can start anywhere**. You don't necessarily have to start at the top and work down. You can start anywhere, but make sure you ask something of your leaders, and give them a means to talk about how they have applied the learning and thereby, amplify their great work, and inspire others.

2. **Involve the wider business**. The more people get involved, talking about what great leadership looks like, talking about who has potential and what they might need to grow and thrive, the more the organization benefits.

3. **Coaching supports growth and accelerates development**. Coaching is a golden thread running through all our programmes and teaching leaders coaching skills and giving them access to a coach themselves, makes all the difference. Leaders need to work on themselves just as hard as they work on projects, tasks and other people.

4. **Don't write people off**. Avoid making assumptions about people and change. Keep an open mind. In my experience it is often the most unlikely people that end up connecting with a subject or technique, and changing the most.

5. **Create unique, memorable, learning experiences** – it makes learning stick and potentially stays with learners for a lifetime.

Which brings me neatly back to the beginning. Being in that audience in 2016, watching young leaders in their element, presenting with passion and integrity. Just like the memory of a great show – it still makes me tingle.

Paul Williamson, MCIPD, is Group Head of Talent Development at ATG Entertainment. He holds a Practitioner Diploma in Executive Coaching from the AoEC and is a member of the Regional Leadership Team for Great Britain, at the Association for Coaching (AC).

IDEAS FOR LEADERS

Academic research in accessible and engaging bite-sized chunks

COMPANIES NEED TO BETTER PREPARE THEIR PEOPLE FOR AI

KEY CONCEPT

Many employees and managers in the workplace fear that they will be left behind as their organizations fail to give them opportunities to learn how to leverage AI in their jobs. Women and managers below senior management levels are at a particular disadvantage.

IDEA SUMMARY

More than half of American professionals use artificial intelligence (AI) in their jobs, according to research from Washington State University's Carson College of Business. The research was based on a survey of 1 200 full-time professionals from throughout the United States.

While 56% of professionals said they used AI in their jobs, that still left a significant 44% of professionals with no AI component in their work. Thirty percent of used AI to analyze data and predict trends, while 24% said they used generative AI to create content or communications.

The support of US companies for AI in the workplace is mixed, according to the study. Twenty-five percent of respondents said their companies were enthusiastic about AI's contribution or potential contribution to their companies' activities, 30% of employers were cautious, 18% were uncertain or confused, and 24% of respondents said their employers did not mention AI at all. Just 4% percent of employers, driven by fear or pessimism, were outrightly negative about incorporating AI in the workplace.

On an individual level, many of the respondents did have concerns about AI, including ethical concerns; privacy and security concerns about organizational, employee, and client data; and/or concerns that AI would be used to make employee jobs obsolete.

Companies are not always helping to alleviate their employees' fears since, the research shows, many are failing to give employees the opportunities to learn how to use AI to improve their performance in their jobs. When asked to describe the AI-related resources their employers were providing, about 1/3 of respondents (32%) said that they had received some general news and resources on AI, while 26% said they had received some information about AI risks and policies. Only 31% of respondents had received specific training on AI tools for their jobs. And nearly a quarter of respondents said their companies had not provided any resources or information at all on the topic.

Looking ahead, about half the professionals believed their companies would train employees if they needed to increase AI expertise in the organization, although some professionals said they expected their company would hire new talent (10%) or outsource (13%) AI expertise. And more than a quarter of employees said they had little idea of how their companies would respond to a need for greater AI expertise.

The research also revealed a gender gap in the availability of AI resources for professionals. More than half (55%) of women said they had received no resources or information about AI. In comparison, just 43% of men said they had received no AI-related resources or information. In addition, while 42% of men had access to mentors or resources to learn about how to use AI in their jobs, only 32% of women received such support.

Not surprisingly, more men than women use AI in their jobs (47% of men compared to 41% of women). In addition, men are more likely to believe that AI can be highly impactful for work in their industry (76% to 68%). Specifically, they are more likely than women to believe that widespread use of AI in their work will improve employee efficiency (64% to 53%) business growth (52% to 43%) organizational competitiveness (53% of 39%), and employee retention (31% to 24%).

The study also shows that senior professionals—the top leadership and upper management of an organization—are more engaged with AI then lower-level professionals. Once again, the study highlights the link between organizational support for AI and professionals' engagement with the new technology: Senior professionals are more likely than their junior counterparts to receive AI resources or information (68% to 36%); more likely to receive resources to learn about how to use AI (48% to 25%); and more likely to use AI in their roles (74% to 40%). As a result, the attitudes of senior leaders towards AI are very different from the attitudes of less senior leaders. Seventy-four percent of senior leaders believe that AI can positively transform work in their industry, compared to just 56% of more junior leaders. Senior leaders are much more likely to believe that AI will have a positive impact on employee efficiency (65% to 30%), business growth (57% to 36%), organizational reputation (47% to 30%) and employee retention (39% to 20%).

BUSINESS APPLICATION

In all industries, artificial intelligence is having a significant impact on how people work and what they do. Yet, according to the study, organizations could do more to prepare and support employees, managers, and leaders in learning to accept and leverage AI in their jobs. The fact that men and senior leaders receive more AI resources and support than women and junior management is a further indictment of the lackluster performance of many organizations in this area. Providing employees and leaders at all levels of the organization with AI training and readiness initiatives is a vital responsibility of any company that hopes to be competitive and successful in the 21st century.

REFERENCES
AI & Business Readiness – 2024. Carson College of Business report (January 24, 2024).
https://business.wsu.edu/ai-business-readiness-2024/

Access this and more Ideas at ideasforleaders.com

ALGORITHMIC DECISION MAKING PREFERRED OVER HUMAN DECIDERS

KEY CONCEPT

Algorithmic decision-making (ADM) is becoming more accepted: A new study reveals ADM is perceived as more trustworthy and fairer than human decision-making. ADM is trusted to make qualitative assessments, a weakness in the past. Finally, negative decisions are more readily accepted by artificial intelligence than by humans.

IDEA SUMMARY

To what extent are we as humans ready to accept decisions made by computers? This was the question at the heart of a study from Michigan State University and Drexel University researchers that examined algorithmic decision-making (ADM) in the context of a job search. ADM, in which machines make predictions, recommendations, and decisions related to human-set objectives, is used in a wide variety of contexts, including employment, health care, and finance. The question remains whether artificial intelligence (AI) can be trusted to make complex and context-sensitive decisions as well as or better than humans.

The study was based on job fit, that is, whether a job applicant was a good fit for the job that he or she was applying for.

At the beginning of the study, participants were introduced to a fictitious online job recommendation service called JobConnect. They then read a job applicant's profile and a job description and determined whether they felt the applicant should apply for the job. Approximately 90% of the participants considered the job applicant qualified.

The participants then reviewed the JobConnect recommendations. Some participants were told the JobConnect recommendations were made by humans, others were told the recommendations relied on an AI algorithm. For some participants, the JobConnect recommendation came back positive (i.e., the job applicant was qualified), for others, it came back negative.

The researchers thus divided the participants into four groups, based on 1) whether the job fit decision was made by a human or by an algorithm, and 2) whether the JobConnect decision was positive or negative (that is, the participant was qualified for the job or the participant was not qualified and should not bother applying).

The design of this study thus allowed the researchers to not only whether ADM or HDM was preferred but also whether the outcome of the decision that is, whether the decision was negative or positive, made a difference in the preference.

In the final phase of the study, the participants were asked to rate the ADM and human decision-making (HDM) on fairness, competency, trustworthiness, and usefulness. They were then asked whether the human or algorithmic decisions had taken into consideration the qualitative and quantitative criteria given in the job description.

Analysis of the results led to three core findings:

1. Participants perceived the algorithmic decisions to be fairer and more competent, trustworthy, and useful than the human decisions.

2. Participants also perceived that the algorithmic decisions took into consideration both the quantitative and qualitative criteria of the job.

3. Finally, participants had a significantly different reaction to a negative outcome when the decision came back that the job applicant was not qualified for the job. Participants were much more likely to accept a negative outcome from the algorithmic decision-maker than from the human decision-maker.

BUSINESS APPLICATION

This study demonstrates the evolution of our perception of algorithmic decision-making. The bottom line: participants in the study had more faith in algorithmic decision-making than in human decision-making. One reason is clear: while ADM would have an advantage in reviewing quantifiable criteria, participants also believe, contrary to expectations, that algorithms can also review qualitative criteria better than humans.

This is a significant finding. In choosing when to use AI-powered decision-making, businesses can be less wary than in the past that ADM is ill-equipped to make qualitative assessments. Another practical implication of the study involves decisions that might elicit negative reactions. It seems individuals will accept a negative decision from an algorithm than from a human. This can be helpful, for example, in feedback situations—since feedback is useful only when the receiver of the feedback is willing to accept it.

The researchers note that they are not advocating a full-scale adoption of ADM in all circumstances. Designers of algorithmic decision-making must continue to improve the capabilities of ADM in terms of contextual decision-making.

REFERENCES
When AI Is Perceived to be Fairer than a Human: Understanding Perceptions of Algorithmic Decisions in a Job Application Context. Hyesun Choung, John S. Seberger, Prabu David. SSRN (In process). https://tinyurl.com/t3j94e5v

Access this and more Ideas at ideasforleaders.com

HOW TO KEEP YOUR AI ETHICAL

KEY CONCEPT

While the significant and positive impact of Artificial Intelligence (AI) on business and society at large is well known, less attention is paid to the potential for unethical applications or outcomes of the new technology. A framework developed by Oxford University researchers offer an action plan for ensuring the ethical application of AI.

IDEA SUMMARY

While the technological capabilities and impact of artificial intelligence (AI) has brought significant change to multiple facets of business and even society, the core of AI is still machines, not humans. And while these machines can learn, they cannot discern right from wrong—unless we deliberately step in to add an ethical dimension to AI. Where to start?

In a report co-sponsored by the Oxford Future of Marketing Initiative and the International Chamber of Commerce, a team of researchers from Oxford University's Saïd Business School review and analyse the academic research in AI ethics, as well as ethical AI-related business statements and governmental and intra-government documents, to develop a framework for maintaining ethical boundaries in the use of artificial intelligence.

The framework's first step is to develop a hierarchical set of principles—hierarchical in the sense that major, overriding principles are broken down into smaller principles.

The two fundamental principles of ethical AI are responsibility, which refers to the processes supported or driven by AI, and accountability, which refers to the outcomes of AI-related activities and operations.

Ensuring accountability begins with proactive leadership, and also includes reporting, contesting, correcting, and liability.

Responsibility is built on a more complex set of components, starting with three key principles: human-centric, fair, and harmless. Human-centric is concerned with the rights and self-determination of individuals, as well as the domains that benefit humans, such as sustainability. Thus, human-centric processes are processes that are transparent, intelligible and sustainable, as well as beneficial. The principle of fairness is achieved though processes that are just, inclusive, and non-discriminatory. Finally, harmless systems are safe, robust, and private.

Using the parameters just described as a guide, the next step in ensuring the ethics of AI applications and use in an organization is to identify where the risks of unethical AI can occur. The first risk 'bucket' is data. For example, the selection of data may be discriminatory or invade the privacy of individuals. The second risk bucket involves algorithms—the set of instructions at the heart of AI that might be influenced by the biases of those developing the algorithms. The final risk bucket is business use, which covers business goals—i.e., AI is used to achieve unethical business goals—and deployment—i.e., users can subvert the original ethical intention of AI towards unethical activities, including activities with adverse societal consequences.

With principles and risks identified, an organization can now take practical steps to ensure the ethical application of AI. The first step is a statement of intent, similar to a mission or vision statement that proclaims the organization's commitment to ethical AI values, policies and practices. The second step is to implement an ethical AI plan for the organization that would include:

1. a specific plan for each application of AI for identifying any ethical concerns and risks associated with data, algorithms and business use;
2. management and mitigation strategies for each risk identified; and
3. a careful record of all actions and decisions related to the identification, management and mitigation of ethical AI risks.

As new risks are discovered or emerge, the original application plans can be updated.

BUSINESS APPLICATION

Borrowing an analogy from its developers, this framework and action plan for applying AI ethically offers both a 'flight plan'—consisting of the ethical AI statement of intent—and a 'flight checklist' for each application of AI in an organization. The checklist allows the organization to monitor and manage the sources of potential ethical issues in its data, algorithms and AI business use, ensuring that AI in the organization leads to outcomes that are human centric, fair and harmless.

It's important to note the dynamic nature of the framework. The vigilant monitoring for potential ethical issues in its applications of AI not only allows the organization to identify problem areas, but also to then put in safeguards and preventive measures, thus increasing the robustness of its commitment to ensure responsible and accountable processes.

REFERENCES
Restorative followership in Africa: Antecedents, moderators, and consequences. Baniyelme D. Zoogah and James B. Abugre. Africa Journal of Management (July 2020). https://www.tandfonline.com/doi/full/10.1080/23322373.2020.1777818

 Access this and more Ideas at ideasforleaders.com

Book Reviews

ChatGPT and the Future of AI

The Deep Language Revolution

By Terrence J. Sejnowski

The MIT Press; October 2024; 264 pages: ISBN: 978-0-262-049-25-2

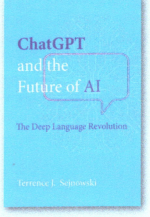

t is always a pleasure, and a rare one, to come across an academic author who is a true polymath, and Terry Sejnowski is a poster-boy example of that (though at 77 he may baulk at that description!). His undergraduate degree was in physics, before shifting to study neuro-biology, his research now focuses on computational biology, with an emphasis on neural networks. His Wikipedia entry also notes he is an adjunct professor in the departments of neurosciences, psychology, cognitive science, computer science and engineering at the University of California, San Diego.

This book is the author's behind the scenes explanation at AI. He notes in the afterword that the media keeps us up-to-date with the latest advances in AI, but few of us understand its foundations. Given the author's wide-range of expertise this book draws together a very wide array of ideas and weaves them into a meaningful tapestry of concepts. Sejnowski fascinates with and spotlights insights across learning, coding, psychology and neuroscience amongst many other disciplines in this guide on how AI has reached its present state – and what we can expect to come next.

The brain is the most complex organ in our bodies, and the more we learn of it, the more we discover it is deeply connected to other organs, so Prof Sejnowski's appreciation of complex connectivity is vital to understanding how all these elements come together, and the outputs they create.

The issue with AI is not so much 'what it can do' but 'how can we best work with it?', and so understanding the human brain and how we operate is key to getting to grips with this.

ChatGPT and the Future of AI is split into three parts. The first describes the current situation with AI; this is a moving target, no sooner is something written on AI than the next breakthrough occurs and we are materially further ahead once again. Nonetheless,

Sejnowski outlines current use-cases, highlighting medicine, education, law, architecture and language/translation examples amongst others... and ingeniously writes his summaries and brief overview enquiries with ChatGPT output.

He also explores the roles of 'priming' and 'prompts' in using ChatGPT. Priming is when you provide context or setting for the LLM, such as 'you are a neuroscientist' or 'you are a friendly and helpful tutor. Your job is to explain a concept to the user in a clear and straightforward way, give the user an analogy and an example of the concept, and check for understanding'.

Prompts are the way you enquire of the LLM for answers. When asked nonsense questions, nonsense answers were returned. However, when prompted to highlight nonsense questions it did so. Similarly, the responses given varied when prompted. Sejnowski points out that LLMs vary in their ability to perform, but asks 'can any human pass all the tests for all professions? LLMs have been around for only a few years. Where will they be in ten years or a hundred years?'

The ability to Prompt well is going to become a key skill, he quotes one such expert: "Good prompt engineering mainly requires an obsessive relationship to language" and understanding how we humans use language is integral to understanding how AI – or 'large language models' behave.

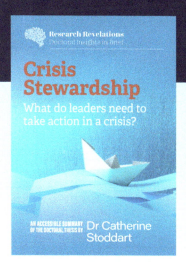
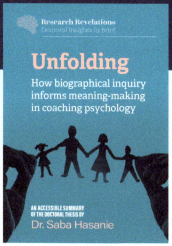

Sejnowski is broadly upbeat about the benefits AI will bring. He doesn't deny that jobs will be lost with the advent of more AI, but he also asks ChatGPT 'What new jobs were created by the introduction of the Internet?' and a string of roles is presented – give it a go yourself!

The second section focuses in on the central element of AI, the 'transformer' (who knew that GPR stood for 'Generative Pretrained Transformer'?). In terms of content to do with leadership this section is relatively unimportant – but in terms of context, and understanding how AI works, it is a goldmine. Everyone should read these 60-odd pages if they truly want to understand how AI functions.

LLMs are fundamentally different to computers (CPUs) in how they work. And our own brains work a million times slower than silicon-based networks, but we have many more synapses/connections than an LLM (currently) does. But for how long? Sejnowski later states that today's LLMs are at the equivalent stage of development as the Wright brothers were in the development of airplanes.

The third section looks to how AI will develop and how we can benefit from that. The goal is Artificial General Autonomy (AGA), which has been described as the prodigy that could rival human thinking, its special power being it actually gets the meaning behind its answers. But we are not there yet. Sejnowski believes that in order to achieve this we need to treat LLMs more like human brains – giving them time to learn from their parents (older LLMs), ensuring 'reinforcement learning' occurs, and that LLMs need to evolve bodies so they can not only do, but also control and sense what they are thinking – pure cybernetics. They also need to extend their interaction memory; currently LLMs start afresh after a finite number of data tokens have been processed (which is why consumer LLMs like ChatGPT can only summarize a relatively small amount of text). This token memory needs to become much larger so it can continue to build its knowledge from prior interaction. Humans memory is significantly processed during sleep in the hippocampus – maybe AGA needs sleep time too. The author notes that 'The new conceptual frameworks in AI and neuroscience are converging, accelerating their progress. The dialog between AI and neuroscience is a virtuous circle that is enriching both fields."

The final section delves deeply into neuroscience and biology and what we can draw from that to show us a way forward with AI. It can get quite technical and loses some of the lightness of touch he displays earlier in the book.

Nonetheless, if you want to get a grasp on how AI has evolved, and where it might take us – there can be few better guides than this book and Terrence Sejnowski.

Leading Through

Activating the Soul, Heart, and Mind of Leadership

By Kim B. Clark, Jonathan R. Clark and Erin E. Clark

HBR Press; September 2024; 272 pages; ISBN: 978-164-7827-61-8

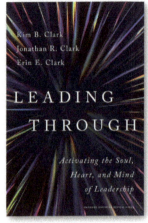

F amily-written business books are rare. Many couples have published novels together, but Kim, Jonathan, and Erin Clark are father, son, and daughter. Kim Clark was dean of faculty at Harvard Business School for 10 years from 1995 until becoming president of Brigham-Young University, where he is a Distinguished Professor of Management.

Jonathan Clark, an associate dean and management professor at the University of Texas at San Antonio, focuses on a version of Ideas for Leaders' definition of leadership: "on helping leaders create the conditions under which individuals, groups and organizations do their best collective work."

Erin Clark, a managing director at Deloitte Consulting – Human Capital, helps clients enhance performance, drive transformation, and gain sustainable advantage through people.

Their work is clearly very aligned across the generations.

Are you happy? Is your workplace full of energy and do you look forward to embracing it every day? Organizations are structured groups of people who align their energies to achieve common objectives, and when they do it well the sum of those individual energies far exceeds its constituent elements. Humanity has advanced because we are skilled at organizing ourselves into collaborative work units to achieve exceptional outcomes.

But if individual energies are not aligned and optimized, the organization's ability to outperform is severely limited. A business that is not optimizing the conditions for its workforce to flourish and thrive is seriously harming its productive potential, particularly in a world where most organizations are knowledge-based, whether that be their product (advice) or management's work to align the parts, or even more traditional work tasks of production.

The authors believe most organizations fail at this, frequently regressing to old top-down command-and-control approaches which bring with them the old disengaged, low productive energy that is now endemic.

This book is about how we can break from this low-energy paradigm, that the authors term Power Over, to a new more invigorating one of Leading Through.

The Clarks say that "when we loosen our grip on consolidated power and control and expand our myopic focus on short-term costs (to prioritize people, purpose, and real productivity) something great – even miraculous – can happen."

The book has four parts: the first compares the Power Over paradigm to the new Leading Through paradigm; the second discusses why Leading Through works and how it affects leaders' souls, hearts, and minds. These are worthy and worth reading, but none of it is really new ground for those who have been immersing themselves in leadership for a while. However, revisiting and revising the essentials helps cement them.

The final two portions of the book uncover how to Lead Through. At the heart of this is the Clarks' concept of leadership modularity. As they explain, modularity is common in manufacturing and tech products, such as laptops and phones, and also in phone apps. But modules also allow for flexibility, innovation, and collaboration among teams, while precise integration specifications can maintain a cohesive whole between modules. "Thus" the Clarks note "modularity promotes freedom and unity."

The rest of part three covers modular leadership system requirements:

- a framework for action
- visible information
- the role of power / power dynamics

The final section discusses how to implement Leading Through. With their modularity focus, they realize that shifting from Power Over to Leading Through paradigms requires incremental change, but all lengthy journeys begin with a single step.

They term their steps as 'touchpoints'. There are seven of them that relate to the six elements of the new paradigm:

- Virtue (the soul / moral context)
- Empathy (the heart / LIVE (Love/Inspiration/Vitality/ Expression) framework)
- Ownership (the mind / leadership process)
- Candor (visible information)
- Respect (power through dynamics)
- Trust and Teaming (framework for action)

Together, these create an organization-wide leadership. Three steps are provided for senior leaders, who can most affect organizational culture. Like all impactful and implementable processes, there is a beautiful simplicity to this – but by clarifying and highlighting it, it makes it much easier to get started:

> **Step 1:** Talk with and listen to people. This colours the context you are operating in and adds detail, it shows your desire to get transformation; it brings others into the conversation; and highlights that change cannot be brought about alone – it needs collaboration
>
> **Step 2:** Establish a baseline. Identify or validate existing values in the organization. Bring in HR and communicate progress across the organization
>
> **Step 3:** Make Progress in the Flow of Work. Nothing will sustain unless it is woven into regular work – and this is the objective here, taking the change from mobilizing to empowering.

Organizations are slowly realizing they need a more nimble, empowered, and purposeful culture to maximize employee energy.

The Clarks' framework of modular leadership is in many ways quite similar to the British Army's Mission Command approach, and it gives us another method to achieve this level of actuation within organizations. It is clearly set-out and readily achievable, all it needs is for senior leaders – and we hope middle managers too – to put it into action.

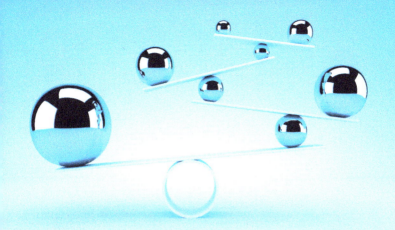

Balanced management begins with reflection

When do your mid-level managers have the chance to stop and reflect on their leadership practice?

Join our growing community of practice once a month for 30 minutes of provocation from a respected thought-leader and 40 minutes of breakout group discussion with other community members from a diverse range of UK organizations.

Upcoming speakers include **Dr Eve Poole on Leadersmithing**; **Prof Maja Djikic on the Possible Self**; **Rebecca Stephens on Stopping, Pausing and Reflecting** – plus enjoy other member benefits - including print copies of DLQ.

For further details visit uk.ideasforleaders.com

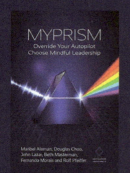

MYPRISM

Override Your Autopilot, Choose Mindful Leadership

Maribel Aleman, Douglas Choo, John Lazar, Beth Masterman, Fernando Morais and Rolf Pfeiffer

Ideas for Leaders Publisher, 2023, ISBN: 9781915529152, 234 pages

Treat problem-solving as a prism treats light: break it down into its component parts.

I Hate Job Interviews

Stop Stressing. Start Performing. Get the Job You Want.

Sam Owens

HarperCollins Leadership, 2024, ISBN: 9781400245895, 224 pages

Banish job interview worries and learn to ace interviews with confidence and ease.

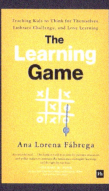

The Learning Game

Teaching Kids to Think for Themselves, Embrace Challenge, and Love Learning.

Ana Lorena Fábrega

Harriman House, 2023, ISBN: 9781804090510, 304 pages

The US education system is failing children. Learn how students can achieve better learning outcomes.

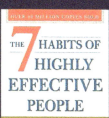

The 7 Habits of Highly Effective People

30th Anniversary Edition.

Stephen R. Covey, Sean Covey and Jim Collins

Simon & Schuster, 2020, ISBN: 9781982137137, 464 pages

To be highly effective, just initiate, focus, prioritize, connect, cooperate, improve yourself and let others win.

ESG Mindset

Business Resilience and Sustainable Growth

Matthew Sekol

Kogan Page Publishers, 2024, ISBN: 9781398614246, 296 pages

Mainstreaming ESG practices in business fosters long-term transformation.

About the Publishers

Ideas for Leaders

Ideas for Leaders summarizes the thinking of the foremost researchers and experts on leadership and management practice from the world's top business schools and management research institutions. With these concise and easily readable 'Ideas' you can quickly and easily inform yourself and your colleagues about the latest insights into management best practice.

The research-based Ideas are supported by a growing series of podcasts with influential thinkers, CEOs, and other leading leadership and management experts from large organizations and small. We also publish book reviews and a new series of online programs.

www.ideasforleaders.com

The Center for the Future of Organization (CFFO)

CFFO is an independent Think Tank and Research Center at the Drucker School of Management at Claremont Graduate University. The Center's mission is to deepen our understanding of new capabilities that are critical to succeed in a digitally connected world, and to support leaders and organizations along their transformational journey.

In the tradition of Peter Drucker, the Center works across disciplines, combining conceptual depth with practical applicability and ethical responsibility, in close collaboration and connection with thought leaders and practice leaders from academia, business, and consulting.

www.futureorg.org

DLQ Advisory Board

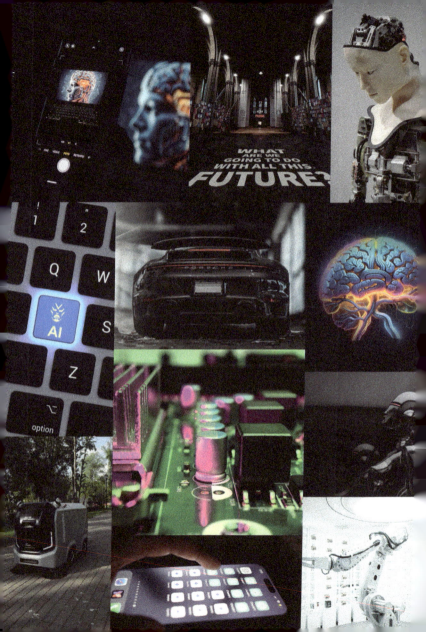

www.ingramcontent.com/pod-product-compliance
Lightning Source LLC
LaVergne TN
LVHW011803070326
832902LV00026B/4621